How to Be Alone
Sara Maitland

MACMILLAN

First published 2014 by Macmillan
an imprint of Pan Macmillan, a division of
Macmillan Publishers Limited

Pan Macmillan
20 New Wharf Road, London N1 9RR
Basingstoke and Oxford
Associated companies throughout the world
www.panmacmillan.com

ISBN 978-0-230-76808-6

9 8 7 6 5 4 3 2 1

A CIP catalogue record for this book is
available from the British Library.

Cover design by Marcia Mihotich
Typeset by seagulls.net
Printed and bound by CPI Group (UK) Ltd,
Croydon, CR0 4YY

SARA MAITLAND is the British author of numerous works of fiction, including the Somerset Maugham Award-winning *Daughter of Jersualem*, and several non-fiction books, including *A Book of Silence*. Born in 1950, she studied at Oxford University and lives in Galloway, Scotland. Visit her website at: www.saramaitland.com

THE SCHOOL OF LIFE is dedicated to exploring life's big questions: *How do we find fulfilling work? Can we ever understand our past? Why are relationships so hard to master? If we could change the world, should we?* Based in London, with offices around the globe, The School of Life offers classes, therapies, books and other tools to help you create a more satisfying life. We don't have all the answers but we will direct you towards a variety of ideas from the humanities – from philosophy to literature, psychology to the visual arts – guaranteed to stimulate, provoke, nourish and console.

Contents

I. Introduction

You have just started to read a book that claims, at least, to tell you how to be alone.

Why?

It is extremely easy to be alone; you do not need a book. Here are some suggestions:

Go into the bathroom; lock the door, take a shower. You are alone.

Get in your car and drive somewhere (or walk, jog, bicycle, even swim). You are alone.

Wake yourself in the middle of the night (you are of course completely and absolutely alone while you are asleep, even if you share your bed with someone else, but you are almost certainly not conscious of it, so let's ignore that one for the moment); don't turn your lights on; just sit in the dark. You are alone.

Now push it a bit. Think about doing something that you normally do in company – go to the cinema or a restaurant, take a walk in the country or even a holiday abroad – by yourself. Plan it out; the logistics are not difficult. You know how to do these things. You would be alone.

So what is the problem? Why are you reading this book?

And of course I do not know the answer. Not in your case, at least. But I can imagine some possible motives:

For some reason, good or bad, of which bereavement is perhaps the bitterest, your normal circle of not-aloneness has been broken up; you have to tackle unexpected isolation, you doubt your resources and are courageously trying to explore possible options. You will be a member of a fast-growing group – single-occupancy households in the UK have increased from 12 per cent of all households in 1961 to nearly 30 per cent in 2011.

Someone you thought you knew well has opted for more solitude – they have gone off alone to do something that excludes you, temporarily or for a longer period; you cannot really feel jealous, because it excludes everyone else too; you are a little worried about them; you cannot comprehend why they would do anything so weird or how they will manage. You want to understand.

You want to get something done – something that feels important to you. It is quite likely, in this case, that it is something creative. But you find it difficult to concentrate; constant interruptions, the demands of others, your own busy-ness and sociability, endless connections and contacts and conversations make it impossible to focus. You realize that you will not be able to pay proper attention unless you find some solitude, but you are not sure how this might work out for you.

You want to get something done – something that feels important to you and of its very nature has to be done alone (single-handed sailing, solo mountaineering and becoming a hermit are three common examples, but there are others). The solitude is secondary to you, but necessary, so you are looking for a briefing. This group is quite small, I think; most of the people who seriously want to do these sorts of things tend to be experienced and comfortable with a degree of aloneness before they become committed to their project.

You have come to the disagreeable awareness that you do not much like the people you are spending time with; yet you sense that you are somehow addicted to them, that it will be impossible to change; that any relationship, however impoverished, unsatisfying, lacking in value and meaning, is better than no relationship; is better than being alone. But you aren't sure. You are worried by the very negative responses you get whenever you bring the subject up.

You are experiencing a growing ecological passion and love of nature. You want to get out there, and increasingly you want to get out there on your own. You are not sure why this new love seems to be pulling you away from sociability and are looking for explanations.

You are one of those courageous people who want to dare to live; and to do so believe you have to explore the depths of yourself, undistracted and unprotected by social conventions and norms. You agree with Richard Byrd, the US admiral and explorer, who explained why he went to spend the winter alone on the southern polar ice cap in 1934: 'I wanted to go for experience's sake; one man's desire to know that kind of experience to the full . . . to be able to live exactly as I chose, obedient to no necessities but those imposed by wind and night and cold, and to no man's laws but my own.' You do not, of course, need to go all the way to Antarctica to achieve this, but you do need to go all the way into yourself. You feel that if you have not lived with yourself alone, you have not fully lived. You want to get some clues about what you might encounter in this solitary space.

You feel – and do not fully understand the feeling – that you are missing something. You have an inchoate, inarticulate, groping feeling that there is something else, something more, something that may be scary but may also be beautiful. You know that other people, across the centuries and from a wide range of cultures and countries, have found this something and they have usually found it alone, in solitude. You want it. Whatever it is. You are reading this book not because you want to know how to be alone, which is perfectly easy as soon as you think about it, but because you want to know why you might want to be alone; why the whole subject fills you with both longing and deep unease. You want to know what is going on here.

But actually the most likely reason why you are reading this book (like most books) is curiosity – why would someone *write* this book?

And I can answer that question, so that is where I am going to begin.

I live alone. I have lived alone for over twenty years now. I do not just mean that I am single – I live in what might seem to many people to be 'isolation' rather than simply 'solitude'. My home is in a region of Scotland with one of the lowest population densities in Europe, and I live in one of the emptiest parts of it: the average population density of the UK is 674 people per square mile (246 per square kilometre). In my valley, though, we have (on average) over three square miles *each*. The nearest shop is ten miles away, and the nearest supermarket over twenty. There is no mobile-phone connection and very little through-traffic uses the single-track road that runs a quarter of a mile below my house. Often I do not see another person all day. I love it.

But I have not always lived alone. I grew up in a big family, one of six children, very close together in age, and in lots of ways a bit like a litter of puppies. It was not a household much given to reflection or introversion – we were emotional, argumentative, warm, inter-active. We did things together. I am still deeply and affectionately involved with all my siblings. I became a student in 1968 and was fully involved in all the excitement and hectic optimism of those years. Then I was married and had two children. I became a writer. I have friends – friendship remains one of the core values of my life. None of this looked like a life of solitude, nor a good preparation for living up a back road on a huge, austere Scottish moor.

What changed was that I got fascinated by silence; by what happens to the human spirit, to identity and personality when the talking stops, when you press the off-button, when you venture out into that enormous emptiness. I was interested in silence as a lost cultural phenomenon, as a thing of beauty and as a space that had been explored and used over and over again by different individuals, for different reasons and with wildly differing results. I began to use my own life as a sort of laboratory to test some ideas and to find out what it felt like. Almost to my surprise, I found I loved silence. It suited me. I got greedy for more. In my hunt for more silence, I found this valley and built a house here, on the ruins of an old shepherd's cottage. I moved into it in 2007.

In 2008 I published a book about silence. *A Book of Silence* was always meant to be a 'hybrid' book: it is both a cultural history and a personal memoir and it uses the forms and conventions of both genres melded into a single narrative. But it turned out to be a hybrid in another way that I had not intended. Although it was meant to be about silence, it turned out to be also about solitude – and there was extensive and, I now think, justifiable criticism of the fact that it never explicitly distinguished between the two. Being silent and being alone were allowed to blur into each other in ways that were confusing to readers. For example, one of the things I looked at in *A Book of Silence* was the actual physical and mental effects of silence – ranging from a heightened sensory awareness (how good food tasted,

Sara's house.

how extreme the experiences of heat and cold were), through to some curious phenomena like voice-hearing and a profound loss of inhibition. These effects were both reported frequently by other people engaged in living silent lives and experienced by me personally in specific places like deserts or mountains. However, a number of commentators felt that these were not effects of silence per se, but of solitude – of being alone. After the book was published I also began to get letters from readers wanting advice . . . and more often than I had anticipated, it was not advice on being silent but on being alone.

Some of this was because there are at least two separate meanings to the word silence. Even the *Oxford English Dictionary* gives two definitions which are mutually exclusive: silence is defined as both the absence of any sounds and the absence of language. For many people, often including me, 'natural noises' like wind and running water do not 'break' silence, while talking does. And somewhere in between is the emotional experience that human-made noises (aeroplanes overhead, cars on distant roads) do kill silence even where the same volume of natural sound does not.

But it was not just a question of definitions. I came to see that although for me silence and solitude were so closely connected that I had never really needed to distinguish them, they did not need to be, and for many people they were not by any means the same. The proof cases are the communities where people are silent *together*, like Trappist monasteries or Quaker meetings.

The bedrock of the Quaker way is the silent meeting for worship. We seek a communal gathered stillness, where we can be open to inspiration from the Spirit of God and find peace of mind, a renewed sense of purpose for living, and joy to wonder at God's creation.

During our meetings for worship some may feel moved to speak: something anyone can do, as all are considered equal. Quakers do not have priests, or a hierarchy, as we believe all people can have a direct relationship with God.

You do not have to be a Quaker to attend Quaker meetings, which are open to all. Meetings can be held anywhere, at any time, although they are often on Sundays in our Quaker meeting houses. If you would like to join us and share in our stillness, you would be most welcome.

(From the official Quaker website, www.quaker.org.uk)

But at a far simpler and less self-conscious level most people have had experiences of being silent but not alone: with someone very intimate, for example, you can be with them for joyful hours without any need to speak; breast-feeding a baby and sitting with someone very near to death are experiences of silence with communion. And equally you can be alone but not silent – for example, if you are watching TV or your neighbours are making an appalling amount of din while you are on your own next door.

There are also less emotionally charged times – if you go for a bike ride with someone, you are often silent and clearly not alone; if you sing to yourself, or call to your dog on a solo walk, you are alone but not silent.

One of my favourite fairy stories is 'The Six Swans': in order to rescue her brothers who have been put under an enchantment and turned into birds, the heroine takes a vow to remain silent for seven years (she also has to make each brother a vest out of flowers). The first half of her labour is done in solitude – she is alone deep in a forest and sits on the branch of a tree to sew. Eventually a king comes riding by, falls in love with her, takes her back to his palace and marries her. They have three children together but she still does not speak. Terrible things befall her but she holds to her vow, until just as she has been bound to a pyre, about to be burned as a witch because of her refusal to speak, the seven years are completed; her brothers are set free from the spell and they rescue her. The heroine has two separate trials – the first is in isolation, and the second, in obvious and deliberate contrast, in a highly social situation – but in both she is silent.

Obviously these two sorts of silence are not the same. But I was still confused, still having a hard job distinguishing them. So, having written a book about silence, I thought I would like to write one about solitude. This is it. I am writing it because I think there is a serious social and psychological problem around solitude which we need to address. I am writing it because I would like to allay people's fears and then help them actively enjoy time spent in solitude. But mainly I am writing it because I like writing books and I like solitude. It is a sort of two-for-one deal for me.

II. Being Alone in the Twenty-first Century

1. Sad, Mad and Bad

There is a problem, a serious cultural problem, about solitude. Being alone in our present society raises an important question about identity and well-being. In the first place, and rather urgently, the question needs to be asked. And then – possibly, tentatively, over a longer period of time – we need to try and answer it.

The question itself is a little slippery – any question to which no one quite knows the answer is necessarily slippery. But I think, in as much as it can be pinned down, it looks something like this:

> How have we arrived, in the relatively prosperous developed world, at least, at a cultural moment which values autonomy, personal freedom, fulfilment and human rights, and above all individualism, more highly than they have ever been valued before in human history, but at the same time these autonomous, free, self-fulfilling individuals are terrified of being alone with themselves?

Think about it for a moment. It is truly very odd.

We apparently believe that we own our own bodies as possessions and should be allowed to do with them more or less anything we choose, from euthanasia to a boob job, but we do not want to be on our own with these precious possessions.

We live in a society which sees high self-esteem as a proof of well-being, but we do not want to be intimate with this admirable and desirable person.

We see moral and social conventions as inhibitions on our personal freedoms, and yet we are frightened of anyone who goes away from the crowd and develops 'eccentric' habits.

We believe that everyone has a singular personal 'voice' and is, moreover, unquestionably creative, but we treat with dark suspicion (at best) anyone who uses one of the most clearly established methods of developing that creativity – solitude.

We think we are unique, special and deserving of happiness, but we are terrified of being alone.

We declare that personal freedom and autonomy is both a right and good, but we think anyone who exercises that freedom autonomously is 'sad, mad or bad'. Or all three at once.

> In 1980, US census figures showed 6 per cent of men over forty never married; now 16 per cent are in that position . . . 'male spinsters' – a moniker that implies at best that these men have 'issues' and at worst that they are sociopaths.
>
> One fears for these men, just as society has traditionally feared for the single woman. They cannot see how lonely they will be. But in time to ease my anxiety, a British friend came through town . . . 'I want to get married,' he said. Finally. A worthwhile man.
>
> (Vicky Ward, *London Evening Standard*, 2008)

In the Middle Ages the word 'spinster' was a compliment. A spinster was someone, usually a woman, who could spin well: a woman who

A woman who could spin well was financially self-sufficient.

could spin well was financially self-sufficient – it was one of the very few ways that mediaeval women could achieve economic independence. The word was generously applied to all women at the point of marriage as a way of saying they came into the relationship freely, from personal choice not financial desperation. Now it is an insult, because we fear 'for' such women – and now men as well – who are probably 'sociopaths'.

Being single, being alone – together with smoking – is one of the few things that complete strangers feel free to comment on rudely: it is so dreadful a state (and probably, like smoking, your own fault) that the normal social requirements of manners and tolerance are superseded.

No one is supposed to be single.

In the course of my life, I have loved and lost and sometimes won, and always strangers have been kind. But I have, it appears, been set on a life of single blessedness.

I haven't minded enough. But now I kind of do. Take dinner parties. There comes a moment, and that question: 'Why don't you have a partner?'

It is usually asked by one of a couple, with always a swivel of the eye to his or her other half, so really two people are asking this question.

And I struggle to answer: 'I have never found the right person . . . I am a sad and sorry manchild . . . I am incapable of love . . . I am a deviant, and prefer giraffes.'

Any answer will fail to satisfy. The questioner expects no happy answer. I am only covering up my bone-deep, life-corroding loneliness. The questioners know this, and the insight they believe it affords comforts them. They are safe.

They look down from the high castle of coupledom, protected from such a fate. But if I were to ask: 'Why have you settled for him? Why are you stuck with her? Were you so afraid of being alone?' such questions would be thought rude, intrusive . . .

Single people can also feel this way about other single people, and about themselves. You see, no one is supposed to be single. If we are, we must account for our deficiencies.

(Jim Friel, BBC online magazine, November 2012)

In both these examples it is clear that thinking the single person 'sad' is not enough for society. Normally we are delicate, even over-delicate, about mentioning things that we think are sad. We do not allow ourselves to comment at all on many sad events. Mostly we go to great lengths to avoid talking about death, childlessness, deformity and terminal illness. It would not be acceptable to ask someone at a dinner party *why* they were disabled or scarred. It is conceivable, I suppose, that a person happy in their own coupled relationship really has so little imagination that they think anyone who is alone must be suffering tragically. But it is more complicated than that: Vicky Ward's tone is not simply compassionate. Her 'fears for these men' might at first glance seem caring and kind, but she disassociates herself from her own concern: she does not fear herself, '*one* fears for them'. Her superficial sympathy quickly slips into judgement: a 'worthwhile' man will be looking for marriage; if someone is not, then they have mental-health 'issues' and are very possibly 'sociopaths'.

Here is a list of the traits of a sociopath, based on the psychopathy checklists of H. Cleckley and R. Hare:

Glibness and Superficial Charm
Manipulative and Cunning
Grandiose Sense of Self
Pathological Lying
Lack of Remorse, Shame or Guilt
Shallow Emotions; Incapable of real human attachment to
    another
Incapacity for Love
Need for Stimulation
Callousness/Lack of Empathy
Poor Behavioural Controls/Impulsive Nature
Early Behaviour Problems/Juvenile Delinquency
Irresponsibility/Unreliability
Promiscuous Sexual Behaviour
Lack of Realistic Life Plan/Parasitic Lifestyle
Criminal or Entrepreneurial Versatility

Does Vicky Ward honestly believe that every un-coupled man over thirty-five is suffering from this serious mental illness? It seems that she does.

Why? Could it be that she is frightened? In her article she comments that, in New York, where she is based, there is an excessive number of single women to men, so if she feels that a committed partner is necessary to a woman's sense of well-being then she might well feel threatened by men who want something different.

Projecting psychopathology onto people who do not agree with you, especially about values, is a very old strategy.

'They are sad and therefore they are mad' is a good cover for fear. There is an alternative, though: 'They are not sad and therefore they are bad.' My mother was widowed shortly after she turned sixty. She lived alone for the remaining twenty-five years of her life. I do not think she was ever reconciled to her single status. She was very much loved by a great many, often rather unexpected, people. But I think she felt profoundly lonely after my father died, and she could not bear the fact that I was enjoying solitude. I had abandoned marriage, in her view, and was now happy as a pig in clover. It appalled her – and she launched a part-time but sustained attack on my moral status: I was selfish.

It was 'selfish' to live on my own *and enjoy it*.

Interestingly, this is a very old charge. In the fourth century AD, when enthusiastic young Christians were leaving Alexandria in droves to become hermits in the Egyptian desert, their Bishop Basil, infuriated, demanded of one of them, 'And whose feet will you wash in the desert?' The implication was that in seeking their own salvation outwith the community, they were neither spreading the faith nor ministering to the poor; they were being selfish. This is a theme that has cropped up repeatedly ever since, particularly in the eighteenth century, but it has a new edge in contemporary society, because we do not have the same high ethic of 'civil' or public duty. We are *supposed* now to seek our own fulfilment, to act on our feelings, to achieve authenticity and personal happiness – but mysteriously not do it on our own.

Today, more than ever, the charge carries both moral judgement and weak logic. I write a monthly column for *The Tablet* (a Catholic weekly magazine) partly about living on my own. One month I wrote about the way a conflict of duties can arise: how 'charitable' is the would-be hermit meant to be about the needs and demands of her friends? One might anticipate that a broadly Catholic readership would be more sympathetic to the solitary life because it has such a long (and respected) tradition behind it. But I got some poisonous letters, including one from someone who had never met me, but who nonetheless felt free to pen a long vitriolic note which said, among other things:

> Given that you are obviously a person without natural affections and a grudging attitude towards others it is probably good for the rest of us that you should withdraw into your own egocentric and selfish little world; but you should at least be honest about it.

And yet it is not clear why it is so morally reprehensible to choose to live alone. It seems at first sight a great deal less offensive than the blatant aggression which the choice seems to provoke in so many people. It is very hard to pin down exactly what people mean by the various charges they make, probably because they do not know themselves. For example, the 'sad' charge is irrefutable – not because it is true but because it is always based on the assumption that the person announcing that you are, in fact, deeply unhappy has some insider knowledge of your emotional state greater than your own. If you say, 'Well, no actually; I am very happy', the denial is held to prove the case. Recently someone trying to condole with me in my misery said, when I assured them I was in fact happy, 'You may think you are.' But happiness is a feeling. I do not think it – I feel it. I may, of course, be living in a fool's paradise and the whole edifice of joy and contentment is going to crash around my ears sometime soon, but at the moment I am either lying or reporting the truth. My happiness *cannot*, by the very nature of happiness, be something I think I feel but don't *really* feel. There is no possible response that does not descend almost immediately to the school-playground level of 'Did, didn't; did, didn't.'

But the charges of being mad or bad have more arguability.

However, before we look at these arguments, the first thing to establish is how much solitude the critics of the practice consider 'too much'. At what point do we feel that someone is developing into a dangerous lunatic or a wicked sinner? Because clearly there is a difference between someone who prefers to bath alone and someone who goes off to live on an uninhabited island which can only be reached during the spring tides; between someone who tells a friend on the telephone that they think they'll give tonight's group get-together a miss because they fancy an evening to themselves, and someone who cancels all social engagements for the next four months in order to stay in alone. Age and circumstance are, or can be, factors, and so is what someone is doing in their solitude: there is a difference between a teenager who has not left their bedroom for four months and an adult who decides to walk the whole Pennine Way alone for their holiday. If you are writing great books or accomplishing notable feats, we are more likely to admire than criticize your 'bravery' and 'commitment'. Most of us did not find Ellen MacArthur sad, mad or bad when she broke the single-handed sailing circumnavigation record in 2005, even though it meant being entirely alone for 71 days, 14 hours, 18 minutes and 33 seconds.

Most of us did not find Ellen MacArthur sad, mad or bad.

There are no statistics for this, but my impression is that we do not mind anyone being alone for one-off occasions – particularly if they are demonstrably sociable the rest of the time – or for a distinct and interesting purpose; what seems to bother us are those individuals who make solitude a significant part of their life and their ideal of happiness.

It is all relative anyway. I live a solitary life, but the postman comes most days. Neil, the cheerful young farmer who works the sheep on my hill, roars by on his quad bike at least three or four days a week, passing with a cheerful wave. I have a phone; I go to church every Sunday. I have friends and children and sometimes they even come and visit me. Small rural communities are inevitably, oddly, social – I know the names and something of the circumstances of every single person who lives within five miles of me. (There is nothing in the world more sociable than a single-track road with passing places.) And even if I lived in deeper solitude I would live with a web of social dependencies: I read books that are written by people; I buy food which is produced by people and sold to me by people; I flick on the light switch and a nationwide, highly technical, constantly maintained, laboriously manufactured grid delivers electricity and my lights come on. It would be both mad and bad not to acknowledge and give thanks for all this not-aloneness.

So it is useful to ask oneself how much solitude it takes to tip over into supposed madness or badness. It is certainly useful to ask those who are being critical or accusatory of anyone who seems to enjoy more aloneness than they themselves feel comfortable with. After all, Jim Friel in the earlier quote is *at a dinner party*, hardly an activity of the classic antisocial loner.

In his book *Solitude*, Philip Koch attempts to break down the accusations into something resembling logical and coherent arguments, so as to challenge them: he suggests that the critics of silence find the desire for it 'mad' (or tending towards madness) because:

Solitude is unnatural. Homo sapiens is genetically and evolutionarily a herd or pack animal. We all have a basic bio-social drive: 'sharing experience, close contiguity of comradeship and face-to-face cooperative effort have always been a fundamental and vital need of man (*sic*) . . . the individual of a gregarious species can never be truly independent and self-sufficient . . . Natural selection has ensured that as an individual he must have an abiding sense of incompleteness.' People who do not share this 'force of phylic cohesion' are obviously either deviant or ill.

Solitude is pathological. Psychology, psychiatry and particularly psychoanalysis are all insistent that personal relationships, ideally both intimate and sexually fulfilled, are necessary to health and happiness. Freud originated this idea and it has been consistently maintained and developed by attachment theorists (like John Bowlby) and particularly object relation theorists (like Melanie Klein) – and is generally held and taught throughout the discipline. (This may also underpin the idea that you are not 'really' happy on your own. Since you need other people to be mentally well, then thinking you are happy alone is necessarily deluded.)

Solitude is dangerous (so enjoying it is masochistic). It is physically more dangerous, because if you have even quite a mild accident on your own there will be no one to rescue you; and it is psychically dangerous because you have no ordinary reality checks; no one will notice the early warning signs.

These three arguments do have a kind of coherence. They are based on assumptions that – were they correct for all people at all times – would indeed need to be answered. I personally think (and I'm not alone) that they are not correct in themselves and do not adequately allow for individual difference. I hope to demonstrate this as we go through the book.

The 'moral' arguments, however, at least as Koch defines them, are rather more absurd. This second group of objections to solitude tend to be exactly the opposite of the first group. Solitude is morally bad because:

Solitude is self-indulgent. The implication here is that it is hedonist, egotistic and seeking its own easy pleasure – that somehow life alone is automatically happier, easier, more fun and less nitty-gritty than serious social engagement, and that everyone in the pub is exercising, comparatively at least, noble self-discipline and fortitude, and spending twenty-six hours a day in the unselfish miserable labour of serving their neighbours' needs.

Solitude is escapist. People who like being alone are running away from 'reality', refusing to make the effort to 'commit' to real life and live instead in a half-dream fantasy world. They should 'man up', get real, get a grip. But if social life is so natural, healthy and joyous as contemporary society insists, why would anyone be 'escaping' from it?

Solitude is antisocial. Well of course it is – that's the point. This argument is tautological. But 'antisocial' is a term that carries implicit rather than explicit moral condemnation; it is clearly a 'bad thing' without it being at all clear what it might mean. All this actually says is 'solitude is preferring to be alone rather than with others/me [the speaker] and I am hurt.' It is true, but is based on the assumption that being alone is self-evidently a bad thing, and being social is equally self-evidently a good thing.

Solitude evades social responsibility. This implies that all of us have something called a 'social responsibility', without defining what that might be or consist of; but whatever it is, for some unexpressed reason it cannot be done by a person who is – for however much of their time – alone.

Now clearly, even here, there are some interesting discussions to be had.

What exactly do personal relationships provide that nothing else can offer? Could, for example, Anthony Storr be right and creative work offers compensatory alternative or even better gratification? Or a sense of meaningfulness? Could some people's peaceful happy solitude function as an antidote, or even a balance, to the frenetic social activity of others? What, exactly, is our social responsibility in a society where most people feel powerless? How does multiculturalism work in terms of individuals as opposed to groups? Why does other people's claim to be happy in a different way from oneself provoke so much anxiety – and why is that anxiety so commonly expressed as judgement, condemnation, rather than genuine concern? How does a society choose which issues it allows itself to be judgemental about, if it has no clear idea of the ultimate good?

And above all, why are these conversations not happening?

I believe they are not happening because of fear. Fear famously paralyses creativity, stultifies the imagination, reduces problem-solving ability, damages health, depletes energy, saps intelligence and destroys hope. And also it does not feel good.

Fear muddles things up; it is difficult to think clearly when you are scared. When we are frightened we tend to project this onto other people, often as anger: anyone who seems different starts to feel threatening. And one problem with this is that these projections 'stick'. As Jim Friel put it in his article, 'single people can also feel this way about other single people, and about themselves'. Of course they can – if you tell people enough times that they are unhappy, incomplete, possibly insane and definitely selfish there is bound to come a cold grey morning when they wake up with the beginning of a nasty cold and wonder if they are lonely rather than simply 'alone'.

In addition there is a contemporary phenomenon which adds to the problem: the mass media make money out of fear.

You may have noticed that the UK experiences waves of grim killer diseases – even though proportionately very few people actually get these illnesses. A successful 'media illness' has to meet quite particular criteria – among other things, it has to have a very complex official name and a very vivid popular one: *Bovine spongiform enceph-alopathy* (and its human counterpart, *variant Creutzfeldt–Jakob disease*) aka mad cow disease was perfect. The illness should also be terminal but rare (CJD only occurs in one in one million people per year, worldwide, and the majority of these cases have no link what-soever with contaminated beef products) so that it is most unlikely that any readers will actually contract it; and if possible it has to be caused by the greed and stupidity of someone else (the food industry and farmers in this case).

Diseases are quite easy to manipulate in order to rack up the right sort of fear – the sort that sells papers. And there are other fears to play on. At the moment a very popular media-inspired terror is the threat of the 'loner'.

Once upon a time, and not very long ago, the word 'lone' had rather heroic and adventurous connotations: the Lone Ranger was not sad, mad or bad; Texas freely and proudly adopted its nick name: The Lone Star State. But recently 'loner' has become media short-hand for 'psychotic mass murderer or sex fiend'. If you look up 'loner' on Wikipedia you will find this alphabetical list of related terms:

Avoidant personality disorder
Autism
Byronic hero
Dysfunctional family
Hermit
Hikikomori
Introversion
Loneliness

Lone wolf (trait)
Major depressive disorder
Misanthropy
Recluse
Schizoid personality disorder
Social phobia
Social rejection
Solitude
Tragic Hero

I have put into italics the four terms which do not directly correlate
with 'sad, mad or bad', although the context of the list raises questions
about even them – is it okay to be 'introverted'? Are hermits actually crazed? Is solitude like Major Depressive Disorder? Are Byronic
heroes lonely? But what are more interesting are the absences: adventurer, sensitive, mystic, creative genius, bereaved, castaway/Crusoe,
victim of solitary confinement, wanderer.

Greta Garbo was a famous loner, though in fact she never said
'I want to be alone' (the Russian ballerina Grusinskaya, whom Garbo
played in *Grand Hotel* (1932), said it). She was a very great actress:
the film historian David Denby wrote in 2012 that Garbo introduced
a subtlety of expression to the art of silent acting and that its effect
on audiences cannot be exaggerated. 'Worlds turned on her move-
ments.' She was sufficiently successful to retire at thirty-five after
making twenty-eight films. Near the end of her life – and she lived to
be eighy-five – she told Sven Broman, her Swedish biographer (with
whom she was cooperating), that 'I was tired of Hollywood. I did not
like my work. There were many days when I had to force myself to

go to the studio . . . I really wanted to live another life.' So she did.

In retirement she adopted a lifestyle of both simplicity and leisure, sometimes just 'drifting'. But she always had close friends with whom she socialized and travelled. She did not marry but did have serious love affairs with both men and women. She collected art. She walked, alone and with companions, especially in New York. She was a skilful paparazzi-avoider. Since she chose to retire, and for the rest of her life consistently declined opportunities to make further films, it is reasonable to suppose that she was content with that choice.

It is in fact evident that a great many people, for many different reasons, throughout history and across cultures, have sought out solitude to the extent that Garbo did, and after experiencing that lifestyle for a while continue to uphold their choices, even when they have perfectly good opportunities to live more social lives. On average they do not turn into schizoid serial killers, predatory paedophiles or evil monomaniacs. Some of them in fact turn into great artists, creative thinkers and saints – however, not everyone who likes to be alone is a genius, and not all geniuses like to be alone.

Greta Garbo; a famous loner.

2. How We Got Here

I am convinced that we need to explore how we have arrived in this odd situation where we are so frightened of being alone that we aggress, or even apparently hate, those who want to be alone. We refuse, as a society, to extend to them the normal tolerance of difference on which we pride ourselves elsewhere. We stigmatize them. We deny their capacity to identify their own emotions. We fret if we do not have 24/7 social connection with others; we go to bizarre lengths to acquire partners (even though we then get rid of them with increasing frequency). I have already said that I believe that fear is at the root of many people's deep unease about, or even terror of, being alone. I want to go further now, and argue that the roots of this fear lie in a very deep cultural confusion. For two millennia, at least, we have been trying to live with two radically contrasting and opposed models of what the good life would or should be.

Culturally, there is a slightly slick tendency to blame all our woes, and especially our social difficulties, either on a crude social Darwinism or on an ill-defined package called the 'Judaeo-Christian paradigm' or 'tradition'. Apparently this is why, among other things, we have so much difficulty with sex (both other people's and our own); why women remain unequal; why we are committed to world domination and ecological destruction; and why we are not as perfectly happy as we deserve. I, for one, do not believe this – but

I do believe that we suffer from trying to hold together the values of Judaeo-Christianity (in as much as we understand them) and the values of classical civilization, and they really do not fit.

The Roman Empire reached its largest territorial extent under the Emperor Trajan, who reigned from AD 98–117. At this point it comprised most of what is now Western Europe and some of Eastern Europe and the whole Mediterranean basin. It was a highly efficient state which spread its cultural and technological influence, as well as its military organization, to its conquered territories. One of the reasons for its success was its unusually cohesive culture, which was based in its original republican ethos of patriotism, citizenship and civic responsibility. Even after the Republic collapsed in 27 BC, when Augustus Caesar became Emperor, these values remained central.

This value system was underpinned by laws which forbade the patricians (the upper classes) to be involved in commerce – this meant that little of their energy could go into 'business' or the accumulation of personal wealth through private or entrepreneurial activities. The young male Roman patrician was educated almost entirely for public office, with a curriculum consisting of rhetoric (public speaking), Roman traditions and public affairs. Such a youth grew up believing that the route to personal 'fulfilment' lay in public life, structured through the *cursus honorum* (literally 'the course of offices'), a sequence of elected roles or 'jobs', which began with serving as an officer in the army and went on through a variety of legal and ceremonial duties up to provincial governor. Although (a bit like the President of the USA) having a lot of money helped you to get elected, you still had to charm the voters. The successful Roman was therefore a public and social figure: that was the ideal. (The word *honorum* originally meant simply 'public office', but you can easily see the connection with the concept of honour. This crossover is still apparent in contemporary Britain in phrases like 'the New Year's *honours* list': where public recognition and status is given to people who are deemed to have performed public services.)

Private morality, interiority and personal 'fulfilment' score rather low in such a culture. Honour meant service to the state, the holding of elected public offices. An honourable person – though in Roman society this exclusively applied to men– was judged through his standing in the eyes of other people. His first moral duty was the appropriate 'performance' of the self in public – generosity, self-control, being law-abiding and a good public speaker were among the necessary qualities. The judgement of your fellow citizens was the measure of your worth. Even bathing was a social event. You were not privately clean, you had to be seen to be clean by your fellow citizens; perhaps unsurprisingly, nudity seems to have carried unusually little shame or embarrassment in Roman culture.

'In men of the highest character and noblest genius there is to be found an insatiable desire for honour, command, power and glory,' wrote Cicero – a man who himself represented and articulated these highest Roman ideals. Marcus Tullius Cicero (106–43 BC) was a statesman, lawyer, orator, political theorist, consul and constitutionalist. He was also a major intellectual, and introduced Romans to Greek philosophy, which further emphasized the social virtues.

Although we now think of Greek philosophy as highly abstract, disembodied and rarefied, it concluded that human nature was essentially social and communal. Aristotle wrote: 'It is strange to make the supremely happy man a solitary, since man is a political creature and one whose nature is to live with others.'

The very word 'civilization' comes from the Latin word *civis* which meant a citizen, just as the words 'polite' and 'political' come from *polis*, the Greek word for 'city'.

But even as this culture reached its greatest height, the Mediterranean world saw the extremely fast rise of a 'new' religion, Christianity, which broke out from its Jewish roots and expanded across the Empire. Christianity proposed a set of values almost directly in opposition to the Roman one. They were distinctly unimpressed by Cicero's 'insatiable desire for honour, command, power and glory'. In fact they were initially sublimely indifferent to politics altogether, since they believed the world was going to end soon and that what mattered was preparing oneself for the immediate return of the Lord Jesus and an apocalyptic final judgement. Their core values focused around a personal (interior) relationship with God and holiness, humility, obedience and poverty. They had a sense of personal integrity which was very unlike the public morality of the Roman world.

For example, they refused to perform the required traditional sacrifice. Actually many Romans did not have any personal belief in their national divinities, but they saw the performance of religious rituals as part of their public duty to the State. What concerned them was good public order. The problem with the Christians was persistent civil disobedience and a deep-rooted culture clash. It is hard to imagine two sets of values – the silent, unworldly (even anti-worldly) Christians and the social, public and political virtues of the Roman world – more radically different. The meteoric success of this innovative cult must have felt extremely threatening to traditional Romans.

Before these tensions could work themselves through and find accommodation with each other, the situation changed totally. In AD 410 the city of Rome fell to Alaric's Visigoth army. The sacking and looting of Rome was a terrible shock to the whole Mediterranean world. There was a deep sense that something had changed forever. Historians still tend to treat 410 as the end of the Classical era and beginning of the Middle Ages.

With the collapse and break-up of the Empire an odd and confusing thing happened. In a highly turbulent and unsettled Europe, broken up into small fragmentary kingdoms and dealing with the constant inflow of new groups of territorially aggressive cultures from the north-east, the Church and particularly the monks – the heirs to the solitary traditions of the desert – became one of the principal forces of social cohesion, continuity and culture. It would be fair to say that of the two competing ideologies of the late Roman period (the public vs the private; the social vs the solitary) the Christian model won, but only by giving up its core values – accepting the 'world', embracing politics, power and even militarism. Western Europe moved into the early modern period with a profound confusion between the values of the social and the solitary; and an unacknowledged but profound belief that people on the 'opposite side' were threatening civilization itself and were therefore very frightening.

The situation was inherently unstable. For the last thousand years, social history has seen a continual seesaw between these two sets of values – and therefore a constant worry and restlessness about how to balance the social communal good against solitary interior freedom.

Until the fourteenth century, solitude was highly valued. The great 'media celebrities' of the period were the saints – and a remarkable number of them were solitary: ascetic monks or hermits; people going into self-imposed exile and rejecting the civilized world; women choosing not to participate in marriage, their only socially conventional lifestyle choice. The greatest virtue was to 'save your own soul' and develop an intimate relationship with the transcendent. Those with more political ambitions (usually kings and would-be kings) could buy themselves out by endowing monasteries and building churches – so that their souls could be prayed for by someone else.

In the fourteenth century the Renaissance, and in the sixteenth century the Protestant Reformation, challenged this dominant paradigm in rather different ways. But the eighteenth century saw a seismic shift. The Enlightenment (or Age of Reason) quite consciously generated a radical shift back towards a more Roman understanding of human society.

The Enlightenment deliberately sought to re-establish the ethics and moral paradigm of the Classical era. This was reflected in many more ways than purely intellectual ones: an aesthetic style evolved which was happily called neoclassicism and affected literature (especially poetry), fashion (men started to wear plain dark clothes and spotless linen neckcloths to demonstrate how chaste and clean they were; women wore simpler, plainer frocks in fragile cottons and fine silks) and particularly architecture, gardening and 'town planning'.

Edinburgh, which self-consciously referred to itself as 'the Athens of the North', built the New Town quite deliberately and knowingly to reflect this understanding of the city as a model of civilization, using classical architecture to represent their rational, civilized, democratic and free society.

Inevitably these changes also affected private morality. The citizen was to be judged by social deportment rather than inner holiness. In *Northanger Abbey* Jane Austen has her heroine, Catherine Morland, weigh the correctness of her actions after a quarrel with her closest friends against such Enlightenment standards:

> She had not been withstanding them on selfish principles alone, she had not consulted merely her own gratification . . . no, she had attended to what was due to others, *and to her own character in their opinion.*

> (Chapter 13, my italics)

For all the era's emphasis on civility, tolerance and liberty, most Enlightenment writers despised solitude, finding it both repellent and immoral. Edward Gibbon, author of the famous *Decline and Fall of the Roman Empire* (1776–88), wrote:

> There is perhaps no phase in the moral history of mankind of a deeper or more painful interest than this ascetic epidemic. A hideous, distorted and emaciated maniac, without knowledge, without patriotism, without natural affection, spending his life in a routine of useless and atrocious self-torture . . . had become the ideal of nations which had known the writings of Plato and Cicero and the lives of Socrates and Cato.

James Wilson was even blunter:

> An ascetic monk or 'self-secluded man', possibly a sulky egotistical fellow, who could not accommodate himself to the

Edinburgh New Town employed classical architecture to represent the city's rational, civilized, democratic and free society.

customs of his fellow creatures. Such beings do very well to write sonnets about now that they are (as we sincerely trust) all dead and buried, but the reader may depend upon it, they were a vile pack.

Sad, mad and bad, in fact!

By the very end of the eighteenth century, however, a new mood began to cut across the refined elegance of neoclassical enlightenment. Ideas of freedom and 'rights' began to conflict with the civic- and social-minded atmosphere; the careful public performance of mannerliness felt restrictive and a sort of anti-Enlightenment developed surprisingly fast into the Romantic movement. Like neoclassicism, it came with both philosophical and aesthetic baggage. Some of the principle ideas included:

- The elevation of emotion over reason and of the senses over the intellect.
- Introspection and the legitimate engagement with the self; a sort of heightened awareness of one's own moods and thoughts.
- A construction of the artist as a free creative spirit.
- An emphasis on imagination and spontaneity as a way to spiritual truth.
- A heightened appreciation of the beauty of nature, particularly in its most sublime and awe-inspiring aspects.

With such a set of concepts it is not surprising that would-be artists had somehow to escape from the coils of social convention and slip back into primal innocence so that they could access their deepest emotions and find their own individual 'voice'. Suddenly there was a plethora of writers praising the value of being alone. William Wordsworth articulated this more explicitly than most in his poem 'The Prelude':

When from our better selves we have too long
Been parted by the hurrying world, and droop,
Sick of its business, of its pleasures tired,
How gracious, how benign, is Solitude.

In a way, this Romantic vision could almost be seen as a return to the early Christian paradigm: the authentic inner self, or true soul, is obscured and weakened by too much worldliness and corrupting materialism. The person desiring perfection must flee into the desert and nurture the inner life in solitude. The difference is, of course, that the idea of God has been replaced by the idea of the ego as quasi-divine.

Through the nineteenth and twentieth centuries this idea extended its reach. Originally it had been understood as a route for 'geniuses', for especially endowed talents, but gradually, as this set of ideas met with wider ideas of equality and human rights, *everyone* became a genius.

This might well have led to a renewal of the values of solitude, but in fact it had, as we know, the opposite effect. This was partly because the concept of freedom and rights had other important dimensions – and many of those required collective actions; among them widening the vote, the trade-union movement, the various campaigns for national freedom (Byron, the great Romantic hero, died in the war to liberate Greece), the struggle against slavery and the two activist phases of the women's liberation movement. These necessarily pulled people into social association and demonstrated the power and effectiveness of collective engagement.

At the same time a general improvement in health, the enormous stresses of increasingly alienated labour and a lowering of inhibition about sex made personal relationships a more important source of pleasure and personal fulfilment. The theme of sexual and emotional satisfaction was picked up as a central issue in the early psychoanalytic movement, so that solitude began to seem not only impossibly difficult but also unhealthy.

Throughout the twentieth century the conflict in values continued. In one sense you could argue that the present model– which emphasizes 'fulfilment' as a 'human right', by widening (but thinning) one's social environment, while seeking the individual good (rather than the communal good) within it – was a clever compromise. But because this model is so brittle, it is inevitably defensive and particularly punitive towards anything that tries to challenge it.

This almost absurdly brisk canter through some elementary history of European cultural paradigms reveals, I hope, a sort of pendulum swinging between various options for understanding the good life; and in all them the question of solitude – both of our psychological capacity and of our ethical obligations to be alone – has been key to the understanding of society and identity. As we came to the beginning of a new millennium, the pendulum was reaching an extreme outer limit of its range, in favour of relationality and social life. This has perhaps been obscured by the cult of individualism, which has, rather oddly, developed simultaneously.

This situation is increasingly fragile. The global financial crisis has raised massive questions about the sustainability of consumerist capitalism based on perpetual economic growth; the language of human rights appears to have delivered just about all the benefits (and they were real and substantial) that it can; people, at least in the developed world, are losing commitment to participatory democracy and to liberal religious faith; and the eco-scientists are showing us with increasing clarity just how tenuous the whole life-as-we-know-it project is becoming. To go back to Rome, the barbarians are at the gate. In these circumstances solitude is threatening – without a common and embedded religious faith to give shared meaning to the choice, being alone is a challenge to the security of those clinging desperately to a sinking raft. People who pull out and 'go solo' are exposing the danger while apparently escaping the engagement.

No wonder we are frightened of those who desire and aspire to be alone, if only a little more than has been acceptable in recent social forms. No wonder we want to establish solitude as 'sad, mad and bad' – consciously or unconsciously, those of us who want to do some-thing so markedly counter-cultural are exposing, and even widening, the rift-lines.

But the truth is, the present paradigm is not really working. Despite the intense care and attention lavished on the individual ego; despite over a century of trying to 'raise self-esteem' in the peculiar belief that it will simultaneously enhance individuality and create good citizens; despite valiant attempts to consolidate relationships and lower inhibitions; despite intimidating efforts to dragoon the more independent-minded and creative to become 'team players'; despite the promises of personal freedom made

III. Rebalancing Attitudes to Solitude

If there is any credibility at all to the somewhat gloomy analysis with which I finished the previous section (and obviously I believe there is), then there is a serious problem confronting us, at least in the developed world. We have arrived at a cultural moment when we are terrified of something that we are not reliably, or healthily, able to evade. Solitude can happen to anyone: we are all at risk. There is no number of friends on Facebook, contacts, connections or financial provision that can guarantee to protect us. The largest, and fastest-growing, groups of people living alone are women over seventy-five (bereavement creates solitude) and men between twenty-five and forty-five (the breakdown of intimate relationships creates solitude). Most often, solitude catches people on the hop, as it were, and few of us can feel we will be securely and indefinitely supported by family, neighbourhood, community or even friendship. It is not sustainable to live in defensive postures of fear and avoidance all the time.

The two most common tactics for evading the terror of solitude are both singularly ineffective. The first is denigrating those who do not fear it, especially if they claim to enjoy it, and stereotyping them as 'miserable', 'selfish', 'crazy' or 'perverse' (sad, mad and bad). The second is infinitely extending our social contacts as a sort of insurance policy, which makes social media increasingly possible.

The first is ineffective because of the risk that a whole range of circumstances may force someone into solitude involuntarily. Should this happen, the fear-and-projection strategy will turn round and bite back: *you* will be the sad, mad, bad person, and this can only make a difficult situation very much worse. Additionally, since – as you will see – there is a good deal of evidence that none of these worries are actually true, people pursuing this route will be obliged to cut themselves off from many ways of knowing about the actual world in which they are living. This itself may well prove isolating: one of the problems with projected fears is that they do tend to make the scary thing or event more likely, rather than less likely, to occur.

The problems with the second option are more complex. In the first place, online social life necessarily entails disembodied relationships. Yet we are a culture that places an extremely high value on sexual and other physical relationships. We understand the limits of language and have an awareness of how much information is carried by non-linguistic communication – by body language, expression and 'tone'. Relationships without these elements are necessarily partial.

Robin Dunbar, Professor of Evolutionary Psychology at Oxford University, argues that there is a neurological limit to the number of people that most human brains have a capacity to perceive as fully developed, complex individuals. Dunbar fixes the number at 150. Michael Hibbert, who claims to have the most Facebook friends in the world, has 8,924. This must, at the very least, change the meaning of the word 'friend'.

In fairness, I should point out that not everyone agrees with me here. There are other reasons for using social media than to generate a plethora of 'thin' relationships.

My friend Anne Wareham the garden writer – someone who definitely knows how to be alone and often is – believes that the New Media creates real communities of choice:

> When we first came to live in the countryside we knew no one. We spent some lonely years building up friendships and those rarely with really like-minded people. And old friends were more difficult to see.
>
> That really was solitude and I remember my frantic efforts to get online when I first heard of the internet and when it wouldn't have offered much anyway – no one there.
>
> But they are there now, and social media introduces you to people around the whole wide world. With Twitter I have met people who share my particular preoccupation with being serious about serious gardens and they are rare – but if you have the world to search you can find like-minded people and they find you. This has also enabled a lively dialogue on the website I edit, www.thinkinggardens.co.uk.
>
> For someone like me, who values solitude, it's ideal. I can manage my time and manage my contact with the world, and give real time and effort where and when I choose.
>
> Now I am conscious that my mother-in-law might perhaps need institutional care one day. She is computer literate and therefore of a generation which may no longer find themselves in the isolation of an institution full of people with nothing in common but age – because they will have the freedom of the web.
>
> It's all an enormous luxury and freedom.

Nonetheless I believe our fear of solitude is real and is in many ways disabling. I do not believe that running away from this reality is effective, protective or even socially beneficial.

So what follows are ideas for overturning negative views of solitude and developing a positive sense of aloneness and a true capacity to enjoy it. It is not progressive – you do not have to do the various exercises in the order I am offering them, but I do suggest that you start with number 1. I recommend starting with the exercises that feel as though they make the most obvious sense to you, and which do not seem too stressful.

Although, as I have said, this programme is not progressive, it is cumulative. Like all learning experiences, you need a combination of theory and practice, so I have tried in the pages that follow to alternate ideas that might strengthen your desire for and reduce your fear of solitude with ways in which you might, in practice, develop your taste for and skill at it.

1. Face the Fear

On the very first page of this book I observed that in a practical sense it is not actually very difficult to be alone. Almost everyone is alone some of the time. So any suggestions for developing a happier relationship with solitude are going to be building on your actual experience. This should be encouraging.

Of course there are people for whom solitude is in reality far more difficult to find than I have implied: for example, the single parent of 2-year-old triplets; people living with some sorts of physical illness, disability or other high-dependency condition; those confined in overcrowded prisons, forced to share a cell; young people with overanxious and controlling parents. But for most of us it is not that complicated. Even those whose circumstances apparently make it hard can refer themselves to Catherine of Siena (1347–1380), who, despite living in a household where there were at least twelve children (her mother had twenty-five babies but many of them did not survive, so the numbers changed frequently) and the family cloth-dying business was carried on, managed to create for herself a 'hermitage of the heart'. 'Build a cell inside your mind,' she instructed someone later, 'from which you can never flee.' Even her family came to recognize and acknowledge that she was a 'solitary'; that she lived alone within that communal household.

If you cannot find *any* regular solitude, any way to be alone, within the rhythm of your ordinary life, then at some level you might be avoiding it; if in addition you feel disgust or contempt towards those who do prefer solitude to company, ask yourself if perhaps you are projecting and scapegoating. These behaviours are classic symptoms of fear.

Although we now use the word 'phobia' (from the Greek: φόβος, *Phóbos*, meaning 'fear' or 'morbid fear') pretty loosely, for psychologists it is a distinct clinical condition. Wikipedia's definition is: 'A marked and persistent fear that is excessive or unreasonable, cued by the presence or anticipation of a specific object or situation.' It is seen as a type of anxiety disorder and has clear diagnostic criteria. Among these are:

1. Exposure to the phobic stimulus almost invariably provokes an immediate anxiety response.
2. The person recognizes that the fear is excessive or unreasonable.
3. The phobic situation(s) is avoided or else is endured with intense anxiety or distress.
4. The avoidance, anxious anticipation or distress in the feared situation(s) interferes significantly with the person's normal routine, occupational (or academic) functioning or social activities or relationships.

Among the clinically recognized 'phobic stimuli' are various aspects of aloneness: autophobia is the fear of being isolated or alone; monophobia is the fear of solitude.

A survey in 2008 suggested that more than 13 million people in the UK have a terror of being out of mobile-phone contact. These individuals experience anxiety and panic symptoms when they run out of battery or credit, lose their phone or have no network coverage. They are suffering from 'no-mobile phobia', which has been given the name *nomophobia* and could affect up to 53 per cent of mobile-phone users.

Of course I am not seriously contending that everyone who cannot enjoy being alone has a pathological psychological disorder, but there some interesting parallels. For example, phobias are often 'learned' or inherited, rather than acquired through a particular traumatic encounter. They have a strong cultural element. The real reason why I am looking at phobias here, however, is because of the ways they can be treated.

The standard, and highly effective, treatment for phobias is a combination of CBT (Cognitive Behaviour Therapy, a popular talking therapy that seeks to change how you think and what you do to help you feel better) and desensitization. Using this as a model, I would suggest that the best treatment for a non-clinical fear of being alone is learning more about it and exposing yourself to solitude, initially in very low 'doses':

Accept the fact that fear is at least one element in your dislike and avoidance of solitude.

Study the benefits and joys of being alone (read this book – and others suggested in the 'homework' section).

Build up various strategies for being alone, starting with the least threatening and most pleasurable ones you can imagine.

- If you can tolerate solitude in the shower – have a bath instead: it takes longer, and because it is quieter it is easier to be aware of being alone. Become more aware of moments of solitude and how they make you feel.
- Spend some time alone where there are other people, but only those not known to you; railway travel is good for this, and so is shopping alone.
- Spend the evening in a different room from the rest of your household.
- Turn your mobile off. Remember, 8 per cent of the adults in Britain – over 5 million of us – do not have a mobile phone. Large swathes of the country do not have even 2G coverage. But life goes on.

Start small.

You may surprise yourself. Once you feel secure in accessing solitude you may find that you like it, and feel its benefits and its joys; you cannot know until you try.

That is what happened to me. I had never lived alone in my life. I had never wanted to live alone. I perceived myself as a deeply sociable, extroverted human being with a particular grace for friendship and highly sophisticated, noisy discussion. When asked, I would say my favourite leisure activity, my hobby, was *deipnosophy* ('the art of or skill in dinner-table conversation'). When my marriage ended and I went to live alone in a little thatched cottage, I was constructing myself as the selfless heroine of a tragic failed love story. I was eagerly anticipating being thoroughly miserable and having one more thing to 'blame' my ex-husband for.

Spend some time alone where there are other people, but only those not known to you; railway travel is good for this.

My subconscious was a great deal smarter than my conscious mind.

I started small. My first home alone was a semi-detached cottage in a small village, barely an hour outside London. My son came up at weekends; my friends visited; for some of the time I had part-time jobs of a distinctly non-solitary kind (I was a writer-in-residence in a prison for two years). So I was only getting small doses of solitude initially. But, for me, it did not take long; I could feel myself relax and expand; I had more energy, both for work and for physical exercise. I got fitter. I slowed down, woke up earlier and started to see the world more sweetly and in more detail. Since I started living alone I have less and less trouble with the depression that I had assumed, throughout my adult life, was a part of my personality.

It took me nearly two years to realize what it was that was making me so happy. Then I got greedier and greedier for solitude: now, as I said, I live in rather splendid isolation in a house designed (by me) for solitary living, in an area where most days I do not see anyone. The joy of long periods of solitude has also increased my joy in non-solitude: I love my children, my friends, my colleagues as much as ever, and I attend to them better when I am with them – and enjoy them more. But, above all, I like me better. I think there is more of me to like – a deep spaciousness of self, joyful, creatively and professionally productive and alert to both my interior and exterior life.

Try it out for yourself. Respect but do not fear your own fear. Do not let it come between you and something that might be deeply enjoyable. Remember it is quite normal to be a bit frightened of being alone. Most of us grew up in a social environment that sent out the explicit message that solitude was bad for you: it was bad for your health (especially your mental health) and bad for your 'character' too. Too much of it and you would promptly become weird, psychotic, self-obsessed, very possibly a sexual predator and rather literally a wanker. Mental (and even physical) well-being, along with virtue, depends, in this model, on being a good mixer, a team-player, and having high self-esteem, plus regular, uninhibited, simultaneous orgasms with one partner (at a time).

Actually, of course, it is never this straightforward because at the same time as pursuing this 'extrovert ideal', society gives out an opposite – though more subterranean – message. Most people would still rather be described as sensitive, spiritual, reflective, having rich inner lives and being good listeners, than the more extroverted opposites. I think we still admire the life of the intellectual over that of the salesman; of the composer over the performer (which is why pop stars constantly stress that they write their own songs); of the craftsman over the politician; of the solo adventurer over the package tourist. People continue to believe, in the face of so much evidence – films, for example – that Great Art can only be produced by solitary geniuses. But the kind of unexamined but mixed messages that society offers us in relation to being alone add to the confusion; and confusion strengthens fear.

One of the best antidotes to fear is knowledge. To press the analogy a little, this is the CBT element that goes hand-in-hand with 'desensitization' in the effective treatment of phobias.

But in reality there is nothing to be frightened of. There is no evidence whatsoever that even prolonged periods of being alone are detrimental to physical or mental health, so long as that solitude is freely chosen.

Unfortunately, in the arena of health, it is quite tricky to find that helpful knowledge: the effectiveness of solitude has not been tested

by NICE and recommended as a – remarkably cheap – NHS thera-
peutic intervention. In *Solitude*, Anthony Storr comments:

> Today, the fact that isolation can be therapeutic is seldom
> mentioned in textbooks of psychiatry. The emphasis is on
> group participation ... [I] regret that the average mental
> hospital can make little provision for those patients who want
> to be alone and who would benefit from being so.

In consequence it is quite hard to find facts and figures on the effects
(negative as well as positive) of solitude in relation to health. 'Being
alone is good for your health' is exactly the sort of proposition that is
singularly difficult to test. You would need a very large-scale longi-
tudinal study, with a control group, to measure anything useful,
because of the problems of eliminating all the random factors that
can so easily sneak in here.

It is not just a matter of 'lies, damned lies and statistics', it is also
about what research gets funded. And in the absence of full, meticu-
lous, controlled experimental research it becomes startling easy for
people to read almost anything they want to into figures.

Here, to put a case that undermines my own, is a statement
about floatation tanks (floatation tanks are devices offered by spas
or alternative health centres, and consist of a 'bath' filled with highly
salinated, body-temperature water, in which the user can float
without effort; they have closed lids and are basically anacoustic –
you bob there in the dark, certainly alone and also deprived of most
sensory input). A tank:

- Promotes total calm, peaceful relaxation, eliminates fatigue and jet lag; improves sleep; alleviates stress – mental and physical; energizes, rejuvenates and revitalizes.
- Stimulates left/right brain synchronization; shifts brain waves from Beta to lower-frequency Alpha, Theta and even Delta; creates mental clarity, alertness; increases creativity, problem-solving; heightens visualization; deepens meditation; expands awareness, intensifies acuteness of all the senses, accelerates learning.
- Enhances hypnotherapy and self-hypnosis; increases motivation, diminishes depression, anxiety and fear; facilitates freedom from habits, phobias and addictions.
- Improves athletic performance and helps prevent sports injuries, speeds healing process.
- Decreases the production of cortisol, ACTH, lactic acid and adrenaline; increases production of endorphins; quickens rehabilitation and recovery; relieves pain – arthritis, migraines, injuries etc.; boosts immune function.
- Improves circulation and distribution of oxygen and nutrients; reduces blood pressure, pulse, heart-rate and oxygen consumption.

I have seen this list quoted in various places as a proof that Floatation is good for you, but there are no citations, no figures, no indication of which 'bit' of the experience is so multiply enhancing. Then it transpires that the original can be found on the website of the Floatation Tank Association – it is an advertisement. Actually I have no reason to believe that any of this is *not* true, and I do appreciate the enormous difficulties that many alternative therapies of all sorts find in getting decent trials up and running. Moreover I am, from personal experience and wide reading, happily convinced that solitude is good for one's health (mental and physical), but in terms of offering authoritative scientific reassurance to counter the common fears, I am not entirely happy with the available data.

Perhaps it is better to approach this question anecdotally, through 'case histories'. Because lives of solitude have been seen by so many different societies as both heroic and bizarre, there is a kind of fascination in solitary practitioners and therefore a fairly steady stream of biographical literature, across a prolonged historical period and from a range of cultures. It is not difficult to find a wide selection of individuals who practised a wide range of solitary lifestyles and simply look and see if there is any suggestion that being alone is dangerous rather than beneficial.

Anthony the Great (AD 251–356) is widely credited as the first Christian hermit, and the founding father of monasticism. In 285 he went out into the Egyptian desert and lived in complete isolation in a ruined fort at Der el Memum (Pispir) for twenty years. Athanasius, his friend and biographer, describes his emergence from this long solitude in some detail. Anthony announced his intention of coming out and sent for some local workmen to help him dismantle his protective 'fortifications'. This attracted a curious crowd who, Athanasius says, were very all very 'surprised' to find he was neither emaciated nor deranged, suggesting clearly that this was the expectation. But he emerged physically fit and eminently in his right mind.

Despite these negative expectations, the rest of Anthony's life seems remarkably sane; and he lived to an extreme old age (105, according to tradition, at a period when life expectancy was much lower than it now is), alone in the desert, still physically and mentally fully active, so his health was evidently not damaged. He spent the five or six years after he left Pispir sharing his experiences and training and organizing the new movement that had grown up around his fort. His success in both establishing a genuinely innovative spirituality and in creating structures that enabled the whole desert-hermit movement to develop over the following three centuries (and expand in an adapted form into Europe and become the basic impulse for monasteries) hardly suggests any serious damage.

After this teaching period he withdrew again into solitude, which he pursued with 'joyful determination' on his so called 'inner mountain'. This second period of solitude, which lasted for the remaining forty-five years of his life, lacked the extremity and rigour of his time in Pispir. He freely met and talked with those who came out to see him, sometimes walked back to visit his community in Pispir and, according to Athanasius, went twice to Alexandria. He was very much loved and respected, partly for his serene good humour and tranquil heart.

Oddly enough, the fact that he remained abundantly normal did not change the common terror that solitude was likely to drive people mad.

Anthony's life-pattern, a period of training, a period of extreme isolation, followed by teaching and public ministry and then a gentler withdrawal into seclusion, has been repeated ever since with surprising frequency and across a range of cultures. Tenzin Palmo is a contemporary example who has followed Anthony's old road.

Jetsunma Tenzin Palmo is a British-born Tibetan Buddhist nun and probably one of the best-known solitaries of our time. She was born in 1943 in Hertfordshire, but moved to India when she was twenty and began training, the only woman in a community of over 100 male monks. She found this, not surprisingly, very difficult, as she felt she was often deprived of both higher teaching and respect because of her gender, and she gradually moved into a life of more solitude. From 1976 she lived for twelve years alone in a cave in the Himalayas, and for the last three of these in complete isolation. Even though her solitude was broken into in an abrupt and potentially damaging way (one day a policeman arrived saying she had twenty-four hours to appear in the nearest town as her visa had expired and she had to leave the country), she appeared unruffled and healthy. She also emerged with a great determination to improve the position of Buddhist nuns. She spent the following years in Europe teaching, lecturing and raising funds for what, in 2000, became the Dongyu Gatsal Ling Nunnery in Himachal Pradesh, India. Again, like Anthony, after this period of teaching and organizing she is speaking again of 'retreat', of going back to her solitary lifestyle.

Like Anthony too she seems marked not just by sanity but by a benign and slightly ironic humour. She appears tolerant, witty and articulate and the many pictures of her show a woman in her seventies in good health and spirits. She is, apparently, an extraordinarily good public speaker and teacher, and continues to work, with considerable success, for the spiritual rights of Buddhist women.

Sadly, a number of individuals embracing a life of radical solitude have gone very mad indeed – like Marguerite de la Rocque, marooned for two years on an island in the St Lawrence Seaway in 1641, who was assaulted and haunted by demons, although she recovered on her return to France, or Alexander Selkirk, the probable model for Robinson Crusoe, who was never able to return to social life after

Tenzin Palmo: Marked not just by sanity but by a benign and slightly ironic humour.

his rescue, and lived in a cave in Scotland – but so have a number of people who have not spent any significant time alone. Overall I can find no evidence whatsoever that there is a higher incidence of lunacy, chronic ill health or early death among the solitary than in the population at large, though I admit that this would be extremely difficult to measure. Although there are intense experiences and sometimes frightening issues to work through, being alone can be beneficial and is certainly not detrimental to well-being, *provided the individuals have freely chosen it*. A good deal of the 'scientific evidence' for the danger to physical and mental health comes from studies of people in solitary confinement. There is no question that compulsory punitive isolation is extremely dangerous to the human psyche – and can lead to a particularly hideous form of psychosis. But to compare freely chosen adventures into the world's wilder places, or the experience of the divine and the depth of the self, to the ordeal of prisoners is a bit like comparing the feelings of a woman pregnant with a wanted baby, basking in support and encouragement, to a woman similarly pregnant but as a consequence of rape, and facing shame and poverty. Of course no one should expect them to feel the same way.

So the biggest danger of solitude is fear – and often fear mixed with both the derision and judgement of others. Those exploring solitude can reasonably anticipate accusations of madness, selfishness and stupidity; and since of course there are going to be elements of all three in all of us, these can sink their barbs in deep, depriving us of joy, confidence and faith; and into the space thus created madness, egotism and idiocy can sneakily enter. Fear is more likely to undermine health than being alone is.

2. Do Something Enjoyable Alone

The most commonly offered reason for not doing something like regular exercise is 'I don't have the time . . .' Often this is a pretty transparent excuse ('I don't have time to go to the doctor, but I do have time to play computer games'). But in fact many of us do live extremely busy and pressured lives, and particularly if we share a home with others, find it difficult to see where yet another clump of hours can be fitted into a life which feels, and perhaps is, already short of them.

This is a genuine difficulty in relation to solitude, because it is too easy to think of it as a 'new' sort of time, which will have to be carved out of other activities. Usually we cannot choose whether we are alone at work, so if we want to experiment with solitude it seems as though it will have to be in our 'spare' or leisure time. But as a society we have constructed leisure as predominantly a communal activity. People who indulge in solitary hobbies are treated as 'odd', if not contemptible: 'geeks', 'nerds', 'anoraks' – trainee 'loners', in all likelihood!

There are some popular leisure activities which cannot be enjoyed alone – team sports are an obvious example, as are Scottish reel dancing, board games and gossip. The activities that can only be enjoyed alone form a smaller but significant group – reading being perhaps the most obvious one. But there are a very large number that can be, and often are, done either in a group *or* alone, like listening to or making music, walking, gardening and watching TV.

It is interesting, occasionally, to look in detail at how one does actually spend one's leisure time – within the working week, during non-working days like weekends and on holiday. Such a list, made honestly, usually shows us just how much time we waste doing nothing in particular at all – 'neither what we want nor what we ought,' as C. S. Lewis described it. But more importantly it reveals that most of us have a pretty clear division between 'work' and 'leisure'. This distinction is a strong feature of post-industrial societies and simply did not exist before that. It is a common belief that so-called 'advanced societies' have more leisure than people used to have – but anthropologists now recognize that hunter-gatherer societies have the most leisure and that 'down time' is one of the biggest losses of modernity. Even in mediaeval Europe the peasant had far more holidays than a middle-class salaried worker has now.

As well as reducing our leisure hours, modern societies have also massively increased the amount of 'maintenance' time we feel is essential for all that washing and cleaning and grooming and decorating – ourselves and our homes. This is partly because we have separated 'work' and 'maintenance': a great deal of necessary maintenance now takes double the time to perform, because first we have to work to earn the money that enables us to do the task. If you are living by subsistence agriculture you might barter to some extent, but you never need to go shopping. It is also partly because over the last couple of centuries we have raised and elaborated our ideas of *necessary* maintenance: far from providing more leisure time, labour-saving domestic devices have made a higher standard of cleanliness obligatory – a daily bath or shower, daily clean underwear, regular changes of bedding, frequent hair-washing and so on – unknown to even prosperous households a century ago.

But the real reason why maintenance takes more time is because we own so many more things, all of which need maintaining. We work longer hours to buy the things, and then we spend more hours managing and looking after them, and so as we become money-richer we also become more leisure-poor.

We are leisure-poor, then, because the combined burden of work and maintenance takes up so much of our time and because we have compartmentalized the three activities. Moreover, in addition to compartmentalizing them in time, we have also divided them in space – we use an increasing amount of our day to move between the locations where the three things take place. There are other ways to be.

I live on a high moor in south-west Scotland. Not much flourishes here except black-face 'free range' sheep. Like many infertile upland areas it got left behind in the years after the 1939–45 war. There was no electricity until 1972; the thirteen miles of un-metalled single-track road between one village and the next had thirteen gates which had to be opened and closed. Each farm was isolated from its neighbours – and most people worked alone. Every summer, though, they had Common Shearing: five or six farms would get together and shear all the sheep, farm by farm; the shearers sitting in a circle on shearing stools, chatting and singing as they worked. The whole family from each farm would come, and whosever farm the shearing was at that day fed everyone. All the older people in this glen remember Common Shearing as a social activity, even though hand-shearing is hard work and an economic necessity. Electricity, as

Even in mediaeval Europe the peasant had far more holidays than a middle-class salaried worker has now.

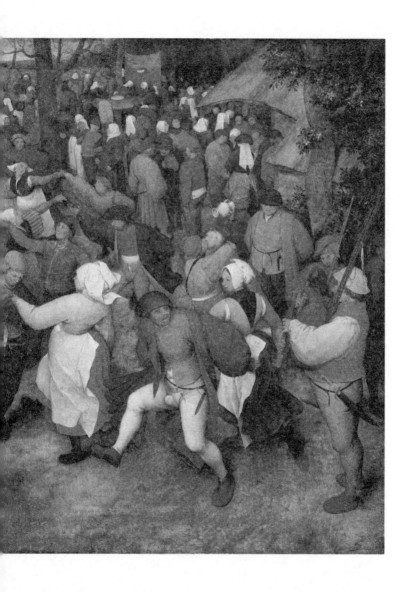

well as a sharply declining population, ended Common Shearing –
power-shears are too fast and also too noisy for sociability. Work and
leisure are no longer seamless.

Life patterns like this have had a long-term influence on our
ideas about 'leisure'. When people worked alone, or with a tiny
and unchanging group like the family, and leisure and work were
more closely entwined than they now are – markets (work) were
also fairs (leisure) – hours spent not alone were social occasions
in predominantly solitary lives. So leisure became associated
with group activities and with sociability. Most of our team and
competitive sports evolved from local and traditional games; much
of our preferred music (the orchestra, the group, the choir) like-
wise emerged from communal activity. Even the word 'holiday' is
derived from the concept of Holy Days, when mediaeval peasants
did not have to perform work duties but did have to go to church – a
profoundly corporate event.

Now most of us do not work alone. We do not even work in
the noisy dangerous places that so isolated individual workers in
nineteenth-century factories. But still when we think about 'leisure'
in our time-stressed, noisy lives, we tend to think of social rather than
solitary activities; and think there is simply no space, once we have
built in work, maintenance and 'leisure', for time to be alone.

This is why it is worth rethinking the leisure you already enjoy
and seeing if there are ways of increasing your time alone within
that framework. This has the additional advantage of relieving some
of the anxiety about solitude by associating it with an activity you
already know you enjoy.

Common Shearing was a social activity, even though hand-shearing was hard work and an economic necessity.

> Running alone can allow you to hit the mute button on the
> world [. . .] and take full advantage of exercise's stress-busting
> benefits. 'Running alone can be a meditative experience
> where you get to really think and concentrate or completely
> clear your mind and zone out,' [a psychotherapist, Michelle]
> Maidenberg says. [. . .] 'You have to practise letting go of
> the inner chatter that can get in the way of what you want
> to accomplish,' [sports psychologist Cindra Kamphoff says].
> 'And that's something you have to do on your own.'
>
> (*Runner's World*, March 2013)

Jogging as a physical discipline was really only established in the
1960s. (1968 saw the first use of the noun 'jogger', in New Zealand.)
This may explain why it is one of the few leisure activities that it is
normal to see people doing alone: it was a response to the symptoms of modernity I have been describing, and so free of the residual
'leisure as social' culture that preceded it. But in fact it is perfectly
possible to do many other activities – outdoors and in – alone: go to
the cinema, an art gallery or up a mountain; fishing, gardening.

Reading and listening to music (or even playing an instrument)
are obvious leisure activities which people do alone; but they do
present an odd question. When you read, are you alone? When you
listen to music – particularly vocal music – is that a solitary activity?
Or is it something you are doing in the company of the writer, the
composer or the singers?

And above all, walking. For me, solitary walking, especially but
by no means exclusively in wilder places, feels like a necessity as
well as a joy. Solitary walking is a profound image of independence

Sara, coming home.

and personal integrity. This makes it a good way to start exploring solitude; it is hard, when walking, not to feel good about yourself and about your capacity to be alone. In addition it is available to almost everyone (you just walk a shorter distance if you are less fit), extremely cheap and embellished with happy associations with creativity, health and pleasure.

There is a good deal of anecdotal evidence that doing things alone intensifies the emotional experience; sharing an experience immediately appears to dissipate our emotional responses, as though communicating it drained away the visceral sensation. I walk a good deal alone and my own experience is that this is very different from walking – even the same walks – in company. I see and notice more and experience both the environment and my physical response to it in a very clear direct way. I also like walking with other people and do that too. The freedom to walk alone, to eat alone, to travel alone, gives at the very least a wider potential pleasure. I would feel deprived if both were not possible for me.

3. Explore Reverie

If you have the opportunity to watch a very young child, who is comfortable and content and neither hungry nor stressed, you can often observe an almost mystical, indescribable expression: the baby's eyes are fixed on some object – very often a loved face – but are also unfocused. The child can take on a Buddha-like appearance – completely intent and completely relaxed. Donald Winnicott believed that the capacity to be alone, to enjoy solitude in adult life, originates in these moments, with the child's experience of being 'alone in the presence of the mother'. (It does not need to be the biological mother who can offer the child this gift.) He postulates a moment in which the child's immediate needs – for food, warmth, physical and emotional contact – have been satisfied, so that there is no need for the infant to be looking for anything; she is free just to be.

Winnicott is describing in psychoanalytical terms what the Psalm writer wrote nearly 4,000 years earlier in spiritual terms:

> See, I have set my soul in silence and in peace;
> As the weaned child on its mother's breast,
> So even is my soul.
>
> (Psalm 131:1–3)

Both Winnicott and the Psalmist are paying attention here to the experience of the child – but reflecting on my own life, I would say that at their very best these rich and lovely moments are entirely mutual. I think that the hours spent thus with my children, especially after the night feeds, were key experiences which encouraged me (literally – gave me the courage) to explore silence and solitude with hope and engagement.

Unfortunately the way most of us were brought up, with an immensely strong focus on stimulation, engagement and interaction, means that too many of us have become adults with no experience of and no capacity for solitude; not because we were neglected or frightened or emotionally isolated but simply because we got no safe practice in our infancy, always being joggled and sung to and dandled and put down and picked up and talked to and interacted with.

As we grew up this continued. Despite the simple fact that the number of abductions and murders of children by strangers has not increased since the 1950s (approximately fifty children are murdered each year in the UK; but over two-thirds of these are killed by a parent or principal carer, not by a stranger) and remains remarkably rare, the fear of it has increased exponentially. This is very odd. It means that even people who can recall how joyful and important time alone was to them as children do not hand this message on to the next generation, but instead wrap the whole idea of solitude in a blanket of anxiety and fear. This increases our nervousness about it, which makes us more reluctant to try it out and often more frightened than there is any need to be.

Luckily there is a 'technique' (if that is the right word) for making good some of this loss. In 1913 the psychoanalyst Carl Jung (1875– 1961), having broken with his friend and mentor Freud and been cut off by the impending war from much of his erstwhile social circle, experienced a sort of breakdown, what he himself described as a horrible 'confrontation with the unconscious', including voice-hearing and hallucinations. He was terrified that he might be becoming psychotic, but bravely decided to confront his fears with a sort of self-analysis. In solitude he worked himself into a state of reverie – a kind of concentrated daydreaming which he called 'active imagination'. He deliberately and as detachedly as possible worked through his own memories and dreams and his emotional reactions to them, and then recorded the sessions in notebooks.

He came to believe that this had proved extremely valuable, and in later clinical practice, especially with older clients, would help people learn to do this for themselves. Because of our contemporary emphasis on object relations (and conceivably because of professional and ego-centred considerations) this 'treatment' has mainly dropped out of the mainstream (although you can get some basic practical advice online if you search for 'self-analysis').

Even without Jung's alarming experiences, *reverie* is a useful way of setting boundaries and patterns to an initial exploration of solitude. One way of using this idea is to place yourself in comfort and safety and then actively seek significant memories of particular states of mind. One interesting feature that psychologists are uncovering is that when people seek moments of happiness, particularly elevated, unitive moments – when the daydreamer uses the active imagination to remember feeling joyfully bound to the whole earth or even universe – they are most likely to be associated with being alone, and often alone outside. Anthony Storr, in *Solitude*, associates this free-roaming solitary pursuit as a particular feature of highly creative people, especially writers. But I myself suspect that it is writers who are best at recording these moments, and that anyone who has had the opportunity to be alone for even relatively brief periods of time as a child can find and re-experience this intense pleasure.

Too often such delights get overlaid by the more social demands of young adulthood, by our own fears of isolation and of being thought weird, and by the culturally inculcated terror of solitude. Reverie is both highly pleasurable in itself and is also a fairly safe way of re-accessing memories.

Most such acts of recall come with a startling vividness – this is one of the ways that people authenticate their own memories. 'It must be true because it feels so complete and satisfying; it must be true because it feels true.' In fact, we now know that memories of childhood are extremely unreliable and are to a large extent confabulations; they are creative acts, constantly in flux and transformation. To me this makes the amazing frequency with which people remember childhood moments of solitude in a positive and often romantic glow all the more interesting. It seems to suggest that as adults many of us have a deep and real longing for more solitude than we are presently getting.

Such practices can, incidentally, throw up quite disturbing material. If this all becomes consistently more frightening than either pleasurable or interesting, it is worth checking whether you are actually exhaling enough (hyperventilation is easy to slip into and produces weird physical effects), and otherwise give yourself a break. I am not proposing this as necessary therapy, but as a rather effective way to enjoy solitude more. If it does not work, does not achieve this end for you, do something different.

4. Look at Nature

By 'look at nature' I do not mean 'get out into nature' – although, as I have already suggested, this is a very good thing to do when you are alone. As I have described, one of the arguments deployed against those who want to be alone is that such a desire is 'unnatural'.

This is a complicated sort of accusation, made up of so many strands that it is quite difficult to unravel and examine it, and indeed it has built itself so deeply into our culture and ways of thought that we seldom even try to unravel and examine it. The word 'natural' has aggregated a confusingly wide range of meanings, some of which are in contradiction to each other. For example, the *Oxford English Dictionary*, along with sixteen other separate meanings for 'natural' as an adjective, defines it both as something 'based upon the innate *moral* feeling of mankind; instinctively felt to be right and fair' and as something 'in a state of primitive development, not spiritually enlightened. Unenlightened, unregenerate.'

Interestingly, until very recently one thing that 'natural' did not mean was 'things like animals, trees, mountains and oceans', although this is often the implication when people call something 'unnatural'. We need to be alert to the implicit and conflicted moral judgement in the word itself because very often when people say something is 'unnatural', they really mean 'I do not approve of it'.

Nonetheless the idea that it is unnatural for human beings to be solitary is very ancient, and still exercises imaginative hold on many of us. When the Pentateuch – the first five books of Scripture which are held in common by the three Middle Eastern monotheisms (Judaism, Christianity and Islam) – was given its final form, some- where between 600 and 400 BC, the second version of the Creation story (Genesis 2) tells how the Lord God made Adam, breathed life into him and put him in the Garden of Eden alone (there were not even any animals at this point) but then came to the conclusion that 'it is not good that the man should be alone'. In an attempt to provide Adam with a fitting companion, the Lord God then 'formed every beast of the field and every bird of the air and brought them to the man'. However, none of them seemed quite satisfactory, so the Lord God made a woman out of one of Adam's ribs. And he was no longer alone. Quite why this one verse of Genesis has kept its resonance while the rest of the creation story has been militantly rejected is a bit mysterious.

This particular story, and its explicit articulation that it is 'not good' for people to be alone, has been extremely influential, but it is not by any means unique; many other creation myths see the forming of human social units (often based on the sexually related couple, though sometimes on a sibling group) as a key moment in human development.

These myths are endorsed by popular science. The idea that human beings are a social species is not simply firmly embedded in our culture; it is supported by evolutionary theory, social anthro- pology and archaeology. And obviously it does have some validity; because of reproduction, virtually no animals can be entirely soli- tary, but there is enormous variety in their sociability. Some species of hamsters, for example, live extremely solitary lives, meeting each other very occasionally and almost exclusively for sex; other species, like ants or termites, are so highly socialized that huge numbers of the members of any particular colony are not even capable of repro- duction but devote themselves to the very highly organized support of their fertile 'queen' and her young. But on the whole, popular 'socio- biologists' do not write bestsellers about termites and hamsters. They prefer more glamorous species.

Most of our closer animal relatives, particularly primates – and specifically chimpanzees, with whom we share a full 98 per cent of our genetic make-up – are social beyond the direct biological needs of feeding, reproduction and child-rearing: they play, groom each other, compete and fight, cooperate, exchange a range of vocalizations and continue to have relationships with their own weaned – even mature – offspring. For most primates their social relations transcend imme- diate family groups. Like humans, it is apparently unnatural for primates to be alone.

Homo sapiens have one particular behaviour that is not shared with other primates – organized hunting. The collective hunt is, inev- itably, a communal and social experience. It has even been suggested that it is hunting as a group that led to the development of language, and the anthropological and archaeological evidence strongly supports the idea that the original human societies were hunter- gatherers. Because of this there has been a tendency to compare ourselves and our social needs to other species who also hunt collec- tively – especially wolves and lions.

But in making the claim that being alone is unnatural because we are fundamentally like other primates and hunting species, it is important to take a wider view of a species' 'lifestyle'.

Lion packs are female-led. However, a newly arrived male lion will kill all the immature offspring of his predecessor. We would not justify such behaviour in human societies on the grounds that it was 'natural'.

Wolves are highly gregarious. But their social groups are organized on entirely familial lines. A pack usually consists of a group of sisters and their young and a single non-related male: if I set up house with my sisters, sharing a single man as a sexual partner and the father of all our children, this would not be seen as a 'natural' relationship.

Nonetheless, the popular argument that it is somehow unnatural for human beings to be alone claims a scientific basis in the behaviours of primates and hunting-pack species. And to some extent this makes good sense: humans have a biological need for sociability, if for no other reason than that it takes so long for our young to become independent; our survival requires us to support and protect these generally pretty useless and vulnerable members, and that in itself needs some sort of social interaction (unlike, say, salmon, whose mothers abandon their eggs before they are even fertilized, let alone hatched). All the archaeological evidence of the earliest human societies, together with the anthropological studies of different societies, make clear that *Homo sapiens* is a social species and cements survival through a complex web of practical, kinship and cultural structures. It is 'natural' for humans to associate, cooperate and bond both emotionally and ritually.

But it is wrong to assume that this necessary sociability, even in the obviously complex forms that exist among primates, means that individuals of other species never spend time alone. This is simply not the case.

Gorillas sleep alone.

Gorillas, for example, despite living in groups, spread out and forage alone. They are capable of a range of vocalizations with distinct meanings – about twenty-five different sounds ('words') have been identified by researchers. One of the most common of these is a loud 'hoot', which can be heard for at least half a mile (0.8 km): obviously you do not need to communicate audibly over such a distance if you are never separate from the rest of your social group.

Gorillas also sleep alone. Each evening they 'make camp', constructing new individual nests either on the ground or in trees. A suckling baby gorilla nests with its mother, but as soon as it is weaned at about three years old, she teaches it to make its own nest and it sleeps there. Many animals sleep together even as adults, but the highly socialized gorillas (and other primates too) sleep by themselves.

Meanwhile orangutans, which are as nearly related to humans as gorillas, are far more solitary in their lifestyle. This species spends most of its daily life alone, although its young are more gregarious.

And not all lions or wolves live in packs: both species have a second form of organizational behaviour – individuals who live alone: the lone wolf and the nomad lion. Both lions and wolves may maintain this status for life, or move in and out of it, setting up new prides or packs. These less-socialized individuals are not rare and are not created by external or unusual traumas – they are, apparently, perfectly 'natural'.

Culturally we like the idea of the close-knit social group, so we tend to ignore how much hunter-gatherer activity is best done alone. The socially organized big-game hunt is surprisingly inefficient: kill-rates vary from as low as 17 per cent up to about 40 per cent, which is not going to keep a community in food. Fishing, small-animal hunting and a great deal of vegetable gathering are frequently done alone. The more northerly, tundra- and taiga-based, hunter-gatherer societies are more dependent on meat, since there is less edible vegetation: their huge and famously complex reindeer hunts are highly socialized and collaborative – different small groups coming together to build elaborate traps and fences and runs to exploit the reindeer-herd migrations. But these spectacular events are seasonal (like the Common Shearing I discussed earlier) and can as easily be seen as 'leisure'; most gathering and hunting and fishing is done more quietly alone.

The more, and the more sensitively, we look at what actually happens out there, beyond the boundaries of modernity – at the complexity of models and forms of social being – the more we will be sceptical about *anything* being purely 'natural' or 'unnatural'. We will most certainly become increasingly aware that solitude, in greater or smaller quantities, is simply a normal part of how it is to be.

5. Learn Something by Heart

This suggestion may come as something of a surprise. What does the tedious, old-fashioned task of rote learning have to do with strengthening your capacity for and enjoyment of being alone? Didn't we break away from that dead educational model decades ago? Now we have the internet, and calculators and mobile phones, why on earth would we want to clog up our brains with those repetitive factoids – like times tables, irregular verbs and the dates of the kings of England?

There are a whole series of counterarguments and answers to these sorts of questions, beginning with the observation that there are other richer things to learn by heart – and note all the connotations of 'heart' here; they include love *and* rhythm. If you find times tables or historical dates boring, learn something else – poetry, a foreign language, the periodic table. But there are two particular answers which relate very closely to the joys of solitude and the fear of being alone: a well-stocked mind enhances creativity, and a mental store of beautiful or useful items offers security, frees one from complete dependence on oneself and appears to aid balance and sanity in solitude.

I have already suggested that solitude may be a necessity, and it is certainly a well-established aid to creativity. One reason why this is so is that the social presence of others distracts or reconstructs a person's sense of their core self. So if, seized with inspiration, you need some material for your creative impulse to work on, you will undermine your own project if you have to turn outside yourself to grasp the necessary information. Wordsworth's famous poem 'Daffodils' would have a very different effect if it ended:

> *For oft, when on my couch I lie*
> *In vacant or in pensive mood,*
> *I have to rise and go and search*
> *On Flickr, Google or YouTube.*

The capacity to be creative is profoundly linked to the ability to remember: the word 'remember' derives from 're-member', to 'put the parts back together'. So strongly was this felt to be the case that classical Greek mythology made Memory 'the mother of the Muses'.

The Muses were the nine beautiful nymphs, the young women who represented the arts and inspired artists: Calliope (epic poetry); Clio (history); Euterpe (flutes and lyric poetry); Thalia (comedy and pastoral poetry); Melpomene (tragedy); Terpsichore (dance); Erato (love poetry); Polyhymnia (sacred poetry); Urania (astronomy). Their father was Zeus, the chief of all the Gods, and their mother was Mnemosyne – memory. We still use the word 'muse' to describe a woman who is an abiding influence on a male artist.

Children's memories used to be trained from primary school, but so-called 'rote learning' has gone out of fashion. A number of people, including me, think this is a pity. There is a good deal to be said in favour of 'learning by heart'.

> The argument in favour of memorizing 'scales or times tables or verse' . . . has been attacked for years now – unfairly . . .

The Muses: Nine beautiful nymphs who represented the arts and inspired artists. Their mother was Mnemosyne – memory.

> Sense and memory are allies ... Rote learning is more like training than learning. It is the trellis on which a free thinker can climb... 'Memorization' used to be almost a synonym for 'culture'. [Now] it is a party trick ... a waste of time ... [Education] 'can only come from the initial submission of the student's mind to the body of knowledge contained within specific subjects.'... In education, submission is empowerment.
>
> (Christopher Caldwell, *Financial Times*, 16 November 2012)

What we have memorized, learned by heart, we have internalized in a very special way. The knowledge is now part of our core self, our identity, and we can access it when we are alone: we are no longer an isolated fragment drifting in a huge void, but linked through these shared shards of culture to a larger richer world, but without losing our 'aloneness'. For many people this resource, this well-stocked mental larder, offers food for thought, for coherence, for security, and must be one of the factors that turns 'isolation' into creative solitude. This is a kind of cultural engagement that you cannot get from the web or from reading.

Another benefit of having a rich and multilayered collection of memorized material ready to hand, as it were, is more anecdotal. Solitary confinement, especially if accompanied by fear, uncertainty or sensory deprivation, really does induce psychosis and lead to the breakdown of even apparently tough individuals. It is therefore worth looking carefully at the individuals who survive such experiences intact; they obviously have an exceptional skill at being alone and we can learn from them. Over and over again this small and admirable group reports the value of having deep-laid, secure material in one's memory-bank.

In 1949 Edith Hajos Bone was arrested in Hungary, where she was working as a journalist. She was kept in solitary confinement – often in the dark, sometimes in the wet, without any recreational facilities (like books or even sewing), subjected to occasional interrogation sessions, and never told what she was charged with or given any information about her future at all: all precisely the features most likely to lead to serious mental breakdown. She survived apparently entirely untouched. She ascribed this to her own mental discipline and intellectual resources. On a daily basis she would walk herself, imaginatively, round cities she had visited; recite poetry – and translate it from one language to another; keep in touch with her own body through the careful medical details she had had to learn by heart as a student doctor. In her autobiography she mentions several other sources of 'amusement', which relied on a well-filled mind: for example, she extracted threads from her towel and wove them into cords:

> One had to be careful not to be caught in the act of pulling threads out of the towel. These were only changed once a fortnight and so it took me about two months to get the required thirty-two threads from which to plait my cord. Fortunately for myself, I had always been a fanatical lover of knots, and possessed that most remarkable publication, *The Ashley Book of Knots*, which I had studied assiduously and which, in addition to knots, also contained a number of sinnets. I plaited a beautiful sinnet – a round one, the sort known as coach-whipping – out of thirty-two threads in groups of eight.
>
> (Edith Bone, *Seven Years Solitary* (Hamish Hamilton, 1957).)

6. Going Solo

Oddly, the form of being alone which attracts least criticism is the one that is in many ways the most dangerous: the solo adventure. It feels strange to me that people who choose to be alone in the comfort of their own house are regarded, and too often treated, as weirdos, while those who choose to be alone several thousand feet above the snowline or in a tiny boat in the middle of Pacific Ocean are perceived as heroes. I am not entirely sure why this is the case; perhaps because so many people do not seem to understand (or to want to understand) what 'being alone' is meant to be *for*, whereas being the first person to do something does strike chords for lots of us. Since almost every square inch of the world has now been explored, doing so under especially tricky circumstances becomes the next new thing.

Circumnavigation is a good example of this phenomenon: in 1522, only eighteen of the 200 sailors, in just one of the five ships which had set out in 1519 under Ferdinand Magellan, returned to Spain. (Magellan himself was killed in the Philippines.) This not-entirely-successful expedition was greeted with extraordinary excitement and enthusiasm throughout Europe. When Francis Drake returned from the second full circumnavigation nearly sixty years later he was welcomed ecstatically and knighted on board his ship, the *Golden Hind*. But after this, circumnavigation became almost commonplace, until the very end of the nineteenth century when Joshua Slocum did it single-handed – alone. In 1969 Robin Knox-Johnston completed the circuit single-handed and non-stop. The challenge to do something new led directly to the need to do it alone.

The same history plays itself out in mountaineering – Everest was first climbed in 1952 by Edmund Hillary and Tenzing Norgay; in 1980 Reinhold Messner was the first person to climb it solo (and without bottled oxygen) and in 1995 Alison Hargreaves was the first woman to make the ascent solo. Both these latter climbers regularly climbed with others – the need to do something not done before pushed them forcibly towards solitary climbing.

The pattern is fairly constant with many other forms of extreme adventure: it is harder to do these sorts of things alone and so it becomes more of a challenge and, for many people, a more heroic endeavour. It also appeals to something almost atavistic in many people who do not themselves want to be alone, and who are often highly critical of people who seek out more tranquil solitude, but nonetheless find solo adventurers deeply romantic and fascinating.

At first sight it appears to be something of a contradiction, but if you want to experiment with being alone it is sometimes easier to do it by making it into an 'adventure' than by staying safely at home. One of the most difficult things about being alone, as I have already outlined, is the distaste and open criticism of one's social circle. If instead of saying 'I'm going to take my holiday alone this year' you say 'I want an adventure; I am going to walk the West Highland Way / cycle to Istanbul / camp on an uninhabited island – solo' you will get all sorts of interest and support. Some of this may be a bit curious or even bemused; people will ask 'why?' But they are far less likely to regard you as sad, mad or bad.

A word of warning: Magellan, Drake, Slocum and Knox-Johnston were all very experienced sailors. Hillary, Tenzing Norgay, Messner and Hargreaves were highly skilled mountaineers. Undertaking extreme adventures without previous experience and knowledge is dangerous – Donald Crowhurst ended up mad and dead in the first Golden Globe race; he had barely sailed single-handed at all when he took his untested yacht out into the Atlantic; Chris McCandless, the 'hero' of the book (and film) *Into the Wild*, almost certainly died from being ignorant and under-equipped. What is a bold adventure for one person is an immature folly for another. In personal terms an 'adventure' is something challenging that you have not done before but have reasonable grounds for believing you could achieve – if you are brave, determined and lucky enough.

Over the centuries a remarkably wide variety of individuals have spoken warmly of the enhanced sense of self they have found in doing something courageous on their own. Henry Thoreau wrote about this sense of empowerment in *Walden*, when he explained why he had gone to live alone in a wood in Connecticut for two years in 1845–47:

> I went to the woods because I wished to live deliberately, to front only the essential facts of life, and see if I could not learn what it had to teach, and not, when I came to die, discover that I had not lived. I did not wish to live what was not life, living is so dear; nor did I wish to practise resignation, unless it was quite necessary. I wanted to live deep and suck out all the marrow of life, to live so sturdily and Spartan-like as to put to rout all that was not life, to cut a broad swath and shave

close, to drive life into a corner, and reduce it to its lowest terms, and, if it proved to be mean, why then to get the whole and genuine meanness of it, and publish its meanness to the world; or if it were sublime, to know it by experience, and be able to give a true account of it in my next excursion.

I do not propose to write an ode to dejection, but to brag as lustily as chanticleer in the morning, standing on his roost, if only to wake my neighbours up.

Richard Byrd, the US admiral and explorer, gave a similar explanation in the opening of his book *Alone*, in which he described his adventure alone through seven months in the Antarctic:

I wanted to go for experience's sake: one man's desire to know that kind of experience to the full . . . to taste . . . solitude long enough to find out how good [it] really was . . . I wanted something more than just privacy . . . I would be able to live exactly as I chose, obedient to no necessities but those imposed by wind and night and cold, and to no man's laws but my own.

If this approach to practising being alone appeals, I highly recommend travelling alone. This is mainly because you almost certainly know how to travel. You will only need to add on the 'alone' bit to turn it into a solo adventure. Tradition says that the mountaineer George Mallory, who disappeared on Mount Everest in 1924 on his third attempt to reach its summit, answered any questions about why he wanted to climb Everest with 'because it's there'. Thoreau and Byrd, along with many others, seem to be answering 'because I am me'. They are doing these things to explore their own inner worlds as much as the external one. Byrd added 'Walking down 5th Avenue can be just as lonely as wandering in the desert – but I contend that no one can be completely free who lingers within reach of familiar habits.'

I have certainly found for myself that solo adventures – of a distinctly more modest kind than these – have given me unexpected and rich material to write about, have deepened my sense of myself as a free and autonomous individual and have provided a quality of challenge and reflection different from anything I have ever been able to achieve at home.

You can also, like the solo adventurers I have just mentioned, build up slowly. It is always less alarming (though less adventurous) to begin somewhere that they speak the same language as you do; what about going to the Orkneys – without flying? The great austere stretch of Scotland north of the Highlands is not only stunningly beautiful, it is little visited and very underpopulated; the landscape itself offers an experience of solitude. Or travel by bicycle to every mediaeval cathedral – adding all the resonance of 'pilgrimage' to your adventure? Or camp out alone, even if it is only in your back garden?

Alternatively you can go somewhere to do something you already know how to do, and like doing: scuba-diving on the Great Barrier Reef, art galleries in New York, shopping in Paris, the opera in Vienna. Travelling in a country where you know no one and cannot speak the language creates particular demands; certainly you will feel more 'alone' when you cannot understand what people around you are saying – no danger of eavesdropping, falling into casual chat or otherwise interrupting one's solitude. But at the same time discovering one's ability to rise to such occasions is even more empowering.

The great austere stretch of Scotland north of the Highlands is not only stunningly beautiful, it is little visited and very underpopulated.

The idea is to push your own boundaries in the expectation of having a new kind of fun. The rewards are a double freedom – the freedom of knowing yourself and pleasing yourself beyond your old comfort zone, and a deeper sense of achievement. You have done something most people are too scared to do. Solo travel gives you both these freedoms, while also usually attracting the admiration and even envy of people who would not dare. Certainly there seems to be an inexhaustible appetite to learn more about solo adventures. There is a huge number of lectures, films, autobiographies, novels and photographs by or about people who have had such experiences. They tend to confirm that individuals flourish creatively and psychologically if they do something that feels courageous to them (and particularly if they have to overcome actual frightening moments) and exciting to others. One thing about 'pushing boundaries' is that they expand as you do so. Beyond these 'beginner' solitudes, the whole world is waiting for you. You may end up feeling, as Thoreau came to feel, that you 'never found a companion that was so companionable as solitude.'

As a society we have a deep belief that travel 'broadens the mind'. If there is any substance in the claim that things you do on your own are experienced more intensely than those that you share with someone else, it seems highly likely that solo journeys will broaden the mind more than package holidays, or even independent travel with a companion.

Most of us have a dream of doing something in particular which we have never been able to find anyone to do with us. And the answer is simple, really: do it with yourself.

7. Train the Children

There is a strong – and I think well-founded – sense that solitude is a learned skill. We know that sociability is culturally acquired: think of all the hours we put in to teaching children to 'share', not to bite each other, to be grateful, to moderate and manage anger and, as they get older, to dress appropriately, not to steal or lie and to consider other people's feelings. No one expects this to come 'naturally' to children, even though we also believe that human beings are genetically programmed for group interaction, are inherently social and *need*, for true flourishing, both to achieve intimate one-to-one relationships and to 'win friends and influence people'. But far from putting similar efforts into encouraging children to develop a healthy capacity to be alone, or to explore what being alone means to them, and to enjoy solitude, we go to extraordinary lengths to 'protect' them from any such practice and experience. I believe that this disables them, or at the very least does not equip them for life events which at some time or another they are extremely likely to encounter.

If you are scared of being alone yourself it can be challenging to allow your children to experience aloneness. We know that being alone is extremely important to some people – and may happen to anyone. We know that solitude is almost a necessity for creativity and the development of a genuinely and richly autonomous sense of identity. We seek out a wide range of experiences for our children –

and want their schools to provide these too. We want young people to develop useful internal risk-assessment abilities, resilience and the capacity to remain strong and well in future difficult situations. We want them to have rich imaginations, physical competence, freedom and as much joy as possible. All these things are enhanced by solitude and by the ability to enjoy being alone sometimes.

There are some strategies for developing these skills in the young. Unfortunately, many child psychologists, and particularly the authors of popular childrearing 'textbooks', have taken the view that a child's psyche is immensely fragile and must be cherished almost obsessively; that any fear is damaging and that children must be protected at all costs from any moment of alarm, even if this means losing out on positive and enriching experiences the other side of that moment of fear. I feel that we, as a society, have allowed our own fear of solitude to affect our judgement and encourage us to advocate ever greater levels of intervention, overprotection, stimulation and social interaction. Some childcare experts, however, have courageously stood out against the tide of fashion: Anthony Storr and more recently Richard Louv, author of *Last Child in the Woods* (2005), are examples worth exploring. However, the following list of ways to give our children safe experience of and practice in solitude, though drawn from their and others' writing, are my own:

1. Allow your newborn time for the infantile reverie I discussed earlier in the book. Let him or her just lie in your arms; do not seek emotional engagement, like eye-contact, immediately. Enjoy for yourself the peace and warmth of being gazed at by your baby. If you cannot

refrain from trying to engage with the child, sing – best of all, wordlessly – rather than talk.

2. Let your toddler play alone sometimes. Do not interfere or make reactive play obligatory. In my experience woods are a very good place to practise elementary solitude. This is because the child can experience herself as unsupervised while you are actually very near. She can vanish behind a tree and believe she is alone, even though she is only a couple of metres away and you can hear every move. Woods are very beautiful and fascinating to small people, while in fact being remarkably safe – there are no real predators, you can hear other people approaching; unlike water, where children really can and do drown, not many bad things actually happen in a wood.

3. Read them stories about children alone, who face real dangers and overcome them. This is the central moral message of classic fairy stories where the hero or heroine, alone and in serious difficulties, turns things to their own advantage by courage and cunning. Many of these stories have endured for hundreds (if not thousands) of years; they must be getting something right. Adults are often scared of frightening their children, but watch a child – they like to be a little frightened, so long as it ends up all right.

4. Remember that it is good for children to be bored sometimes. Children who are not continually provided with stimuli develop more active imaginations, a stronger sense of self-sufficiency and, probably, higher self-esteem.

5. Delay as long as possible giving them their own mobile phone. If there is a practical need on specific occasions, or they are doing something that makes you anxious, then lend them one.

6. Never use isolation ('go to your room') as a punishment. They will not be in a mood to use their solitude positively and they will associate being alone with being bad and unhappy. Instead, if you are able to provide them with space of their own, offer them 'time out' as a reward.

7. Only interrupt a child engaged in a solitary activity (reading, solitary hobbies, loafing about outside) if you have a clear and specific reason which you can articulate. ('You have to come in now because it is supper time' vs 'Darling, are you all right out there alone?')

Our children are not happy. I believe this is because over the last half century we have increasingly monitored, supervised and attended to them, and pampered their supposedly frail egos. The original motivation for this was deeply benign, but the sorry fact is that it is not working. We have an increasing number of children with diagnosable mental health issues (10 per cent of children between one and sixteen is suffering from a diagnosable mental 'disorder' at any given time); we have too many children with pathetically short attention spans; we have profoundly alienated youths, who seem to have remarkably poor judgement and serious issues with personal risk assessment, who do not trust adults and do not choose to engage with them. In 2007, a report from UNICEF ranked the UK bottom in childhood wellbeing compared to other industrialized nations.

Woods are a very good place to practise elementary solitude.

In 2009, a survey of 16-to-25-year-olds by the Prince's Trust found 1 in 10 believed that 'life was not worth living'.

These figures are terribly sad. We are doing something wrong. I am not, of course, suggesting that more solitude for young people would solve all these serious, and indeed tragic, problems instantly, but given the known, beneficial effects of solitude already discussed in this book it might be worth giving them a chance to try it. For me, two important issues are that solitude in childhood appears to be an almost universal experience of creative people and that children love being frightened in a generally safe context (that is why fairgrounds remain in business).

Children, like grown-ups, need different amounts of direct stimulus, company, social engagement and time alone. Neither you nor they can know which sort of person they are if they cannot ever try out solitude.

8. Respect Difference

Bernard Shaw once said, 'Do not do unto others as you would have them do unto you; they may have very different tastes.'

How much solitude does a person need? There is no real answer to this, because everyone is different. There is a helpful vocabulary for anyone trying to think this through, although recently it has got clogged up a bit – the language of Introversion and Extroversion.

Based on Carl Jung's 1921 definition of personality 'traits', a whole system of analysis has developed around the question of how much solitude people want or need. The suggestion (and there are various 'explanatory' theories, ranging from cortical stimulation to childhood expectation and experience) is that there are two distinct types of people, who process stimulation differently. For example, in one set of defining qualities you have statements like:

Extroverts are 'action' oriented, while introverts are 'thought' oriented.

Extroverts seek 'breadth' of knowledge and influence, while introverts seek 'depth' of knowledge and influence.

Extroverts prefer more 'frequent' interaction, while introverts prefer more 'substantial' interaction.

Extroverts recharge their energy by spending time with people, while introverts recharge their energy by spending time alone.

Unfortunately it has proven extremely difficult to create a satisfactory way of testing who is which in any very useful way. This is partly because most people do not have a single consistent style of responding, but are more introverted or extroverted in different contexts or moods, and partly because it has proved nearly impossible to find a testing method which is not heavily culturally biased. 'Do you enjoy going to parties?' is based on the Western assumption that there are parties of a particular type to go to, whereas in some countries gathering in groups may not perform the social function of 'parties' at all. (For example, going to church, a social gathering that is enjoyable to most of the participants, and often noisy with singing and dancing, may well be a 'party' for some individuals or cultures and not for others.)

So some psychologists have claimed that happiness is a matter of possessing three traits: self-esteem, optimism and *extroversion*, and that studies prove that extroverts are happier than introverts. However, these findings have been questioned, because the 'happiness prompts' given to the studies' subjects, such as 'I like to be with others' and 'I'm fun to be with', only measure happiness among extroverts!

Furthermore, even if extroversion makes people happier, this might be because Western Europeans, and especially Americans, live in an 'extroverted society' that rewards extrovert behaviours and rejects introversion. Extroverted societies have been described as validating a 'culture of personality', whereas other cultures are 'cultures of character' where people are valued for their 'inner selves and their moral rectitude'. These cultures, such as in Central Europe or Japan, prize introversion. And it transpires that in such cultures introverts report greater happiness than extroverts! This is not as twisted as it looks: it makes people feel happy to be approved of.

There are two social tendencies which further complicate this: the first is the apparent irresistible desire to move these sorts of words from adjectives to nouns. So someone with strongly introverted inclinations becomes 'an introvert'. This divides and separates people from each other and traps people in boxes. ('She is a blonde', 'he is a homosexual' and 'they are disabled' are other examples where a single characteristic comes to define the person; they may all be true, but they do not describe the fullness and complexity of most individuals.)

The other social tendency that goes with this is the universal difficulty we all have with difference itself: the principle of 'different but equal' is almost impossible for people to maintain without effort – once you have created this sort of binary system, almost everyone instinctively gives higher value to one or other of the 'differences', usually the one with which they most comfortably associate themselves. There is a nice example of an American church leader urging congregations to appoint pastors who scored high on extroversion tests because 'of course Jesus was an extrovert'.

Sadly, then, although the idea that introversion and extroversion are both normal variants of behaviour ought to help us accept ourselves and understand others, it does not always have this effect.

Moreover we should not really need a complicated psychological test-kit to say something so simple. Individuals are different – and we value difference and individuality rather highly in our present society. We would very properly resent government policies designed to make us all exactly the same, insisting for example that we all wore identical uniforms or listened to the same music. It is reasonable and normal then that people should like different amounts of solitude. Even those people who never want any at all should respect those who do – and vice versa – and indeed, as fellow human beings, try to understand why and appreciate the different values that ought to enrich us as a society. It is interesting, but beyond my brief, to wonder why this is so hard: all of us want to be treated as complex and unique human beings, but simultaneously want everyone to be just like ourselves.

Used carefully and discriminatingly, avoiding the temptation to absolutize the sets of behaviours, and understanding the limits of the terms, I do find thinking about these psychological 'tags' can be useful. If nothing else, the words can be used to open up conversations about how much solitude, quiet and social withdrawal different individuals need: 'Do you think of yourself as more extroverted or introverted?' is quite simply a more interesting and less-rude question than 'Why are you single?' or 'Why are you so antisocial?'

And asking people why they like being alone or what they get out of it (and of course listening to their answers) is one very effective way of learning about being alone and enjoying it.

IV. The Joys of Solitude

So now it is time to look more closely at the benefits and indeed the 'bliss' of solitude. I am going to turn to the positive claims that have been made for being alone and see if I can persuade you that they are worth pursuing.

Over the centuries during which people have explicitly practised solitude and reflected on their experience (that is, as long as we have had any form of recorded human culture) there have been surprisingly consistent reports of what it might offer those who seek it out. These 'rewards' can be grouped into five categories, although they overlap and are certainly not exclusive:

1. A deeper consciousness of oneself.
2. A deeper attunement to nature.
3. A deeper relationship with the transcendent (the numinous, the divine, the spiritual).
4. Increased creativity.
5. An increased sense of freedom.

What seems to me most worth noticing is how widespread, through both time and social arrangements, these experiences are. They are not some mad aberrations of a single, or even a few, heroic or crazed individuals. Very different people, alone for very different reasons and using very wide-ranging images and languages, all say fundamentally similar things. Going by their example, you might try seeking these rewards of solitude yourself.

1. Consciousness of the Self

In his excellent and informative book *From the Holy Mountain* (Flamingo, 1998), William Dalrymple tells a delightful and revealing little story. Dalrymple was staying with a Coptic monk in the Egyptian desert, and he questioned the hermit about his motivation for choosing such an austere lifestyle.

> 'Many people think we come to the desert to punish ourselves, because it is hot and dry and difficult to live in,' said Father Dioscuros. 'But it's not true. We come because we love it here.'
>
> 'What is there to love about the desert?'
>
> 'We love the peace . . . You can pray anywhere. After all, God is everywhere, so you can find him everywhere. But in the desert, in the pure clean atmosphere, in the silence – there you can find *yourself*.'

Exactly what this 'self' might be remains, of course, *the* continuing philosophical (and psychological and spiritual and intellectual) question. If the self is just 'me', how can 'I' lose it – or for that matter find it? Nonetheless, over and over again people write of solitude that it allows them to 're-gather' a sense of self that can get 'scattered'. Oliver Morgan, quoting from Koch's *Solitude* (see Homework for details), uses the image explicitly:

I can sense that my 'person' is pulling back from its scattering into the details and plans of today, like a wave rolling from sand and shore back to its ocean source – collecting itself into a unity of 'ocean'. 'I' am here, present to myself and available for a possible revelation of what is inside me . . . I am present too for experiences of those guiding, inner images (personal metaphors, archetypes) that I sense shape my values, actions, judgements and decisions during the rest of the time.

Thomas Merton, from a religious angle, sees this process as morally necessary:

All men need enough solitude in their lives to enable the deep inner voice of their own true self to be heard at least occasionally. When that inner voice is not heard, when he cannot attain to the spiritual peace which comes from being perfectly at one with his true self, his life is always miserable and exhausting . . . If a man is constantly exiled from his own home, locked out of his own solitude, he ceases to be a true person.

But you do not need to be so grandiose about this business of knowing the self; it is not just a truth for reflective philosophers or great minds. It can be quite domestic and ordinary. Here my friend Jill Langford describes what joy solitude gives her and how she goes about getting it in a very busy life:

About twenty-five years into my marriage, with seven children, I asked my husband for a one-man tent for Christmas.

A little taken aback, perhaps, he nonetheless granted my request and bought me a super little army tent or bivouac shell that you honestly couldn't squeeze two people into. You erect it, quite easily and quickly, crawl in on your belly, then turn over onto your back, clutching a sleeping bag, raise your knees and wriggle your legs, then bottom, then torso into it. Et voilà. You stay in that position till morning, then you do the same in reverse. There is no room to sit up and you'd be a fool not to have a wee before retiring, since the whole procedure is well-nigh impossible in the middle of the night.

I use this little tent just whenever I feel the need to take off, alone, for whatever reason. For me, it works like a battery charger when I feel weighed down by the burdens of living in community and am dragging my feet. Actually I don't use it very much, but knowing it's there to use if I want to is sometimes enough in itself to bring a spring back into my step.

When I do need to use it, I find it best to have a car handy, since there is nowhere to store any kit inside the tent and in my part of Scotland it's usually raining. The car is good because it gets you far from home quickly, so no one will come tramping across the fields to find you until you are done with being alone. This usually takes two full days, but a single night would be better than nothing.

The first morning, emerging from your bivouac-thing, there is a great sense of joy and freedom. You feel quite alone in the world and no one knows who you are or why you are there. You could be in a campsite surrounded by happy families or out in the wild woods with silent, dumb creatures that creep and crawl. It makes no difference, the point is that you are alone because you wanted it this way. You don't talk to a soul the whole time. You just get up, brew a coffee on a camping stove and then zip up the tent and go. It doesn't really matter where you go either. You know that you have about twelve hours ahead of you just to yourself. So you start walking, along the coast, up a hill, by a river, down a valley, anywhere, on and on, stopping every now and then for a banana and a drink (massive water bottle) and a sit.

It feels good. You find yourself skipping, no, gambolling, like a newborn lamb. In your head, details about daily life swiftly give way to songs, hymns you used to know, praise, yes praise, for God's mind-blowing creation. Your thoughts then turn to God because there aren't any people about and you find yourself chatting amicably with Him. Sometimes there are tears, sobbing even, but this comes with emptying. It's really all about emptying. And then, renewal. This is what we miss if we don't empty stuff.

By nightfall, the little tent and sleeping bag beckon: you greet them both joyfully and shut down. Usually it's freezing and sleep comes in patches, but the night time wakefulness is all part of it. You use it to set things straight, mentally.

Another day ahead, more wanderings, then hunger sets in and you head for home, refreshed.

This sort of experience, this kind of rediscovery of one's own self and its unique delights, just on its own seems a good reason for experimenting with a little solitude: if nothing else, it is a great deal cheaper than a therapist!

2. Attunement to Nature

I love this word 'attunement' to describe a widely shared sense that there is something crucial about solitude in relation to an engagement with nature. It is not my word, but Philip Koch's, in his book *Solitude*, where he explores this attunement and breaks it down into three different components:

1. Clear, undistracted, sensitized perception.
2. Symbolic perception: perceiving nature as signifying or symbolizing other things.
3. Fusion/interfusion: the loss of the sense of barriers between oneself and nature, the sense of flowing out into it as it simultaneously flows through oneself.

When I wrote *A Book of Silence* I came up with an almost identical list, except that I saw them as effects of silence rather than solitude. But I have come to think that Koch may be right; nature is seldom, if ever, really silent.

The first of Koch's list is, in a sense, fairly obvious. Nature is reclusive or 'shy'; if you want to see, you have to pay careful attention and you have to go quietly – and both these things are much easier to do alone. I have found that even having a dog as a companion means that I see less – the birds fly away and my attention is less focused. You are more likely to perceive clearly if you are undistracted. Being alone is known to intensify all physical sensation. But there is something more to it. A great many people find they agree with Henry Thoreau that 'it appears to be a law that you cannot have a deep sympathy with both man and nature. Those qualities that bring you near to the one estrange you from the other . . . The mind that perceives clearly any natural beauty is in that instant withdrawn from human society.'

The business of finding meaning, or metaphor and symbol, in nature seems an almost atavistic reaction. The gods of our ancestors were, on the whole, gods of the wild places; very small children can be entertained for hours finding images in the shapes of clouds, and the poet Wordsworth writes tragically of his character Peter Bell:

A primrose by a river's brim
A yellow primrose was to him,
And it was nothing more.

It is less immediately clear why being alone so powerfully enhances this capacity – perhaps because there is no one to express a different symbolism, to challenge your meanings with theirs, so that the effect of your meaning can sink deeper into the mind.

The experience of fusion with, or into, nature is, when it happens, one of the highest joys of solitude. In *A Book of Silence* I describe one such episode on the Isle of Skye:

I climbed up the steep-sided corrie. It was sheltered there and magnificent – almost vertical mountains on both sides

– a mixture of shining rock and loose scree, and below, tiny stands of water that looked like handfuls of shiny coins tossed casually down. It was so huge. And so wild and so empty and so free . . . And then quite suddenly and unexpectedly, I slipped a gear or something like that. There was not me and the landscape, but a kind of oneness: a connection as though my skin had been blown off. More than that – as though the molecules and atoms I am made of reunited themselves with the molecules and atoms that the rest of the world is made of. I felt absolutely connected to everything. It was very brief but it was a total moment.

Over and over again individuals report these extraordinary, mystical experiences when they are alone in nature. It never seems to happen if you are with anyone else, perhaps because we all have a deep inhibition against exposing ourselves so nakedly to another, even a beloved other.

3. Relationship with the Transcendent

For me personally, the transcendent is God. It is the desire for an ever more intimate relationship with God that drives my own desire to be alone, and many of the great solitude-seekers have had a similar passion. It was this that led the early Christian hermits out of their cities and into the enormous solitude of the desert; and later drove the Irish hermits to seek out tiny islands across dangerous seas, like Columba of Iona. But the search for solitude is not confined to Christianity. From the earliest traditions, Buddhists, who do not identify a 'God' in the Western sense, have nonetheless – more than anyone else, perhaps – used solitude and silence as a vehicle of transcendence, and have evolved a massive 'how-to manual' to support that practice.

In fact there is no major (and I do not know of any minor) religious or spiritual tradition that does not recognize solitude as a part of the necessary practice for revelation, intimacy and knowledge. This would suggest that those who desire an experience of the transcendent might look to a range of these well-worked traditions to see what they are up to, and how to achieve that experience of transcendence. But the state of joyful consciousness beyond the limits of the personal, the framework of the ego, does not require a religious framework.

It would appear that a period of being alone is a prelude to initiation of many kinds. We know that Moses, Buddha, Jesus and Muhammad all spent periods in solitude before launching their religious missions.

We know that what the Tibetan Buddhist nun Tenzin Palmo has called the 'pressure cooker' of solitude and retreat is normally (though there are exceptions) a necessary precursor to intense religious experiences, especially those we usually called 'mystical'.

In many societies throughout the world a period of solitude is seen as a necessary part of such ritual initiation, and especially for rites of passage – those ceremonies which mark the transitions from one social status to another. Many Aboriginal youths, for example, are sent out into the desert, alone, for up to six months in some cases, to fend for themselves, before they can be deemed to be adults. Other societies arrange other kinds of seclusion for these crucial times of transition. For example, the Takuna of the north-west Amazon see the time when a young woman starts to menstruate as being particularly perilous; they have created a complex ritual, the *Festa das Mocas Novas* (the Feast of the New Women), which both protects and celebrates the event.

This ritual happens when a girl first menstruates; for somewhere between four and twelve weeks, she lives alone in a little room specially built inside the family home, which represents the underworld, where she is hidden from dangerous demons called the Noo. As the rite reaches its climax guests arrive wearing masks to impersonate the Noo and the girl is painted with black dye. She remains in the chamber and after three more days, under the protection of her family, she is led out to a celebration and dances all night, until dawn. She is then given a flaming brand by a shaman to throw at the Noo; their demonic power is broken and the girl is deemed to be an adult woman.

In mediaeval Europe both religious people (monks and nuns) and men about to become knights passed the night preceding their initiation in a 'vigil', awake but alone in preparation for their initiations.

These sorts of experience are not by any means limited to religious contexts, although socially recognized rituals probably make it easier to access the emotional states of transcendence. Bernard Moitessier, the single-handed yachtsman mentioned in Part III, seems to have loved being alone at sea mainly because it brought on these experiences of intense unitive awareness of transcendence. The poet Samuel Taylor Coleridge used to stand on the very edge of cliffs to provoke vertigo, which gave him a direct sensation of the transcendent (this is not a method I would advocate). John Muir, the pioneer early conservationist and inspiration behind the National Parks movement, describes poising himself on the very edge of an enormous waterfall in order to feel its power and glory. For him this clearly went beyond the 'attunement to nature' I discussed in the previous chapter, and opened a way into mystical experience very close to religious ecstasy.

Because rites of passage are found in almost all societies, and take such an extraordinary variety of forms – not all of them necessarily including solitude or exclusion from the group – it is difficult to generalize about what is going on or why this is so crucial to the human psyche. But this sense of meeting or encounter between transcendent powers and the individual, alone, in liminal space, is so pervasive that it is hard not to trust to such universal wisdom.

John Pettie's 'The Vigil': A squire prepares himself for life as a knight on the eve of his knighting ceremony.

4. Creativity

'Conversation enriches the understanding, but solitude is the school for genius,' wrote Edward Gibbon.

Of all the claimed rewards of being alone, this is perhaps the easiest to 'get'. It seems rather obvious that great art, great original thinking, any creative work, needs to be done in some degree of solitude. What is more, all the creators tell us so – from Franz Kafka to William Wordsworth; from Werner Heisenberg to Beatrix Potter; from Georgia O'Keefe to Ludwig Wittgenstein (just to take a tiny range). It seems a universal truth, and it mirrors our own smaller experimental performances. But actually it is slightly odd, because, as Anthony Storr puts it, 'Art is communication . . . explicitly or implicitly the work which [is produced] in solitude is aimed at somebody.'

We seldom inspect this paradox, because the reality is so self-evident. Kafka wrote to his fiancée:

You say you would like to sit beside me while I write. Listen, in that case I could not write at all. For writing means revealing oneself to excess, that utmost of self-revelation and surrender . . . that is why one can never be alone enough when one writes . . . why even night is not night enough.

(You may not be very surprised to learn that, shortly after this, they broke off the engagement!)

The poet Rainer Maria Rilke advised a younger poet,

> What is needed is . . . a vast inner loneliness. To walk in one's self and to meet no one for hours on end. That is what one must be able to attain . . . looking out from the depths of one's own world from the expanse of one's own aloneness which is itself work and rank and profession.

In *A Room of One's Own*, Virginia Woolf argues very convincingly that the reason there were so few great women writers is that it was so difficult for them to be alone: a writer needed a room of her own and enough money to occupy it. Women were not lacking in talent, intelligence, energy or imagination – they were lacking in solitude, in the chance to be alone for long enough to be creative. Later Woolf goes on to try and work out why solitude mattered so much to creativity. She suggests that every woman is haunted by a sort of inner ghost, which she calls 'the angel in the house' (after a Victorian poem of that name by Coventry Patmore extolling his wife as the ideal woman). Woolf describes the perfect woman as

> intensely sympathetic. She was immensely charming. She was utterly unselfish. She excelled in the difficult arts of family life. She sacrificed daily. If there was a chicken, she took the leg; if there was a draught she sat in it . . . Above all, she was pure.

Emily Dickinson: Great original thinking, any creative
work, needs to be done in some degree of solitude.

This angel-ghost prevented a woman from doing anything so assertive and 'aggressive' as truly creative work. But Woolf goes on to suggest that this 'angel' was a social construct (in the interests of husbands, fathers and men more generally) and an imaginative projection. In order to 'kill the angel', which Woolf considered both necessary and difficult, you had to get away from all the people who were projecting, were constructing the would-be writer, not as writer but as an 'intensely sympathetic', 'pure' and 'unselfish' woman. To get away from them all you had to be alone.

At first sight this might seem to apply only to women – and certainly the 'angel in the house' is a peculiarly female problem – but I think that perhaps everyone, even the notably introverted Kafka, is haunted by an inner ghost who undermines creativity by implying that there are better things to do with your time, asking sarcastically who you think you are and preaching modesty and humility and 'unselfishness', or the social duty to get rich, help other people and be a good team-player or other social obligations. If these are really social constructs which we have internalized they tie very neatly into our society's negative views about solitude: the two reinforce each other.

It is difficult to create any solid theory about the human imagination, how it is triggered into action of any kind, and what might be done to develop and strengthen it. But anecdotally, and in almost all biographies of creative artists and scientists, periods alone seem to be crucial.

Werner Heisenberg wrestled for some years with the theoretical question of how to model the atom to take into account the mathematical problems which seemed to distort all the data. He talked at length with his friends and other experts; they seemed to get nowhere and he was intensely frustrated. And then in 1925 he had the 'good luck' to suffer a violent attack of hay fever; to recover from this he went off on his own to Heligoland (an island in the North Sea, famous for its absence of pollen). And there he was alone. And alone he came up, very quickly, with his Theory of Imprecision (now normally called the Uncertainty Principle). It was a profoundly creative piece of physics, and it challenged and inspired many of the people whom he had been talking to beforehand. It opened the door for one of the most creative few years that modern physics has ever known: Quantum Mechanics sprang into existence because of Heisenberg's hay fever and the solitude it imposed on him.

If you feel any identification with Heisenberg's frustrations, in any creative area, you do not need to have a major allergic reaction; you can just go off on your own and see if it helps. Solitude is a well-established 'school for genius', and the outpouring of creativity is one of its promised joys. In learning to be solitary and happy with it, you can prepare yourself for this sort of creativity.

life is and can become'. That is to say, you need a consciousness of yourself, and we have already seen how solitude enhances and develops that self-awareness which is the first step towards being self-governing.

But it goes further than this. There is a very real sense in which the presence of other people limits our personal freedom. At the very crudest level most of us do not feel 'free' to pick our noses or fart in company. A little further up the social scale, even in these libertarian times, many places of business still require workers to wear a uniform and most have an implicit, if not an explicit, 'dress code'. Even party invitations suggest what you might want to wear – and most people find this helpful, even though it is of course a restriction. Even if you decide not to abide by the advice, your complete freedom to dress as you choose will have been compromised. On the whole, people in a group feel most comfortable when they are, broadly speaking, conforming to the behaviour of that group. When my ex-husband and I separated, our houses very quickly diverged in decor – while we lived together I did not feel consciously inhibited, but the first room I decorated in my own, single-person, household was a colour I would not even have thought of before. We did not fight about the colour of the walls, but I learned (and judging by his present house, he also learned) to pre-compromise when we came to make those kinds of choices. Now I know I like jewel-bright colours to live with. Being with each other, in this small and not very important way, restricted our personal freedoms. It is inevitable, and in any good relationship an acceptable price to pay, but we should not disguise from ourselves that there is a price.

Because there is another more profound sense in which being alone strengthens personal freedom. Assuming that you are a reasonably nice person, who finds it easier to feel happy and confident when those around you – and especially those you love – are happy, then some of your energy and imagination is bound to be (and should be) engaged in their happiness as well as your own. R. D. Laing, the radical psychiatrist, wrote a little monologue to show the way in which love itself – desiring the good of the beloved other – can make personal choice and freedom extremely complex. Here the 'speaker' (a fictional voice) wants to be happy but sees that those around her are not:

They are not having fun.

I can't have fun if they don't.

If I can't get them to have fun, then I can't have fun with them.

Getting them to have fun is not fun. It is hard work.

I might get fun out of finding out why they're not having fun.

I am not supposed to get fun out of working out why they're not.

In fact this sense of knowing yourself alone and nakedly, so to speak, may be one part of why solitude inspires creativity – because creating something yourself, of your own, uniquely, requires a kind of personal freedom, a lack of inhibition, a capacity not to glance over your shoulder at the opinions of others.

Nonetheless, it is oddly the case that life with others seems to work more smoothly when individuals do know what they want, even if they are prepared to compromise it for the greater collective enjoyment. Nothing is more destructive of warm relations than the person who endlessly 'doesn't mind'. They do not seem to be a full individual if they have nothing of their own to 'bring to the table', so to speak. This suggests that even those who know that they are best and most fully themselves in relationships (of whatever kind), need a capacity to be alone, and probably at least some occasions to use that ability. If you know who you are and know that you are relating to others because you want to, rather than because you are trapped (unfree), in desperate need and greed, because you fear you will not exist without someone to affirm that fact, then you are free. Some solitude can in fact create better relationships, because they will be freer ones.

Here is Alice Koller again, summing up these points:

> Being solitary is being alone well: being alone luxuriously immersed in doings of your own choice, aware of the fullness of your own presence rather than of the absence of others. Because solitude is an achievement.

V. Conclusion

I chose to write this book back-to-front. It is more usual with this sort of 'handbook' to begin with all the glories and delights of your subject and only move on to the problems and more negative details once you have whipped your readers up into a state of joyful anticipation. I've done it the other way round. This is because, although I myself love being alone and want other people to enjoy it more, I am very aware that this is a bit countercultural in our present society. So I decided to get all the negative stuff out of the way first and keep the benefits and delights of solitude until those that needed it were reassured and so that readers could finish the book on a joyful high.

There are many joys of solitude but in this book I have outlined those that seem to me the most obvious and open to everyone's experience. If even one of these five rewards or benefits of being alone has content for you – and it generally appears that in fact they come together to a considerable extent – then it is worth overcoming any fears or doubts you may have about embracing the freedom and at the very least trying out some personal solitude and seeing what happens. It is an adventure.

Homework

The following pages include ideas and books to help you think further about solitude.

I. Introduction

There are two important theoretical books about being alone: rather annoyingly they are both called *Solitude*. One is by Anthony Storr (Flamingo, 1988) and looks psychoanalytically at solitude, loneliness and creativity, and concludes there are other routes to fulfilment and psychic well-being than intimate relationships; creative work may satisfactorily replace these. (The book was originally titled 'School for Genius'.) The other is by Philip Koch and is subtitled 'a Philosophical Encounter' (Open Court Publishing Co., 1994). Both are deeply affirmative and helpful.

Perhaps the most famous book about being alone is by Henry Thoreau. Thoreau (1817–1862) was a nineteenth-century American author, poet, philosopher, abolitionist, naturalist, tax-resister, surveyor, historian and leading transcendentalist. In 1856 he published *Walden*, which is an account of the two years he spent living alone in a hut in a wood near Concord in Massachusetts. It has become a major classic, and together with Wordsworth's 'The Prelude' – and much easier to read – it is the great book linking solitude and nature.

Isabel Colegate has written a lovely history of hermits called *A Pelican in the Wilderness* (Harper Collins, 2002). She defines 'hermits' in non-religious terms, but most of her subjects take a fairly extreme path of solitude. Peter France's *Hermits: insights of solitude* (Chatto & Windus, 1996) is more focused on prayer and spirituality, but is beautifully written and illuminating about what people have gained from being alone through the centuries.

Richard Byrd (1888–1957) was a US admiral, early aviation adventurer and explorer. His book *Alone* (Shearwater Books, 2003; originally published 1938) describes his time alone in Antarctica. This expedition was not altogether successful: a faulty stove leaked carbon monoxide into his hut and he became seriously ill. The attempts to rescue him take up a good deal of the book. However, before he got sick he wrote some of the most beautiful prose about the beauty and solitude he found there. It is an inspiring read.

The figures from the 2011 Census for the UK have now been published by the Office of National Statistics in various forms, both online and print. They make a fascinating background to many discussions, including those contained in this book. Here is a pie chart showing the numerical size of households:

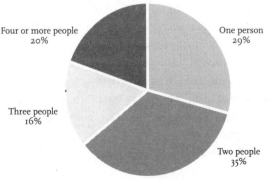

Notice how large the segment of single-person households is. It is not odd to live alone. Pin this graph up somewhere visible and if you find the idea of 'being alone' alarming, look at it and take comfort from the knowledge that you will not be alone in being alone!

Quakers (more formally called the Society of Friends) are a religious denomination founded in the seventeenth century. They are famous for their commitment to pacifism, their refusal to take oaths, their radical stand on a wide variety of issues, their complete lack of a leadership structure and their 'meetings for worship', which are predominantly silent. There will be a Quaker Meeting near you, and if you are uncertain whether it is silence or solitude you are most in search of, you might well find some clues by attending one. You will be made welcome and not pressured to 'join'.

Trappists are an order of Roman Catholic monks who live under a 'reformed' version of the Rule of St Benedict, which incorporates a great deal of silence. The monks communicate in a form of simplified sign language. Thomas Merton (1915–1968) was a Trappist and *The Seven Storey Mountain* (published in the UK as *Elected Silence*, Hollis & Carter, 1949) describes the life of the monks. There are no Trappist monasteries in the UK, but there are various contemplative (more or less silent) orders, especially of women, and it is possible to visit many of them. Making a private visit, often called a 'retreat', is a very safe and structured way to experience being on your own, although surrounded by experts and well looked after. Most such communities welcome visitors; you do not have to be a Christian and will not be required to attend services. There is a comprehensive list of retreats available at www.retreats.org.uk.

My own *A Book of Silence* is published by Granta. Although, as I say, it is more about silence than about solitude per se, it is more or less impossible to write about one without writing about the other and it contains very full references to a great many books and individuals who have practised the two together.

II. Being Alone in the Twenty-first Century

1. *Sad, Mad and Bad*

James Friel is a novelist. His most recent book, *The Posthumous Affair*, was published by Tupelo Press in 2012. He teaches creative writing at Liverpool John Moores University. He lives alone.

In the third and fourth centuries thousands of Christians went off to be hermits in the desert – mainly in the Egyptian desert, but also in Sinai, in what is now Syria and in Jordan. It was perhaps the first large-scale experiment in being alone that we have any record of. These hermits are often called the Desert Fathers, although some of them were women. They were quite experimental – trying out a variety of forms of prayer, ways of supporting themselves, ascetic disciplines and lifestyles. They had enormous influence on subsequent Christianity, because monasticism, as it developed in the West, was based on their practices. As they were much admired by their contemporaries, their stories and reflections were collected in several different books. Anyone worried about solitude and sanity should read some of these 'sayings', as they are called. The most admired of these hermits tend to be gentle, generous, humble, kind and slightly self-mocking. There are many translations of these originals. I particularly like the tone of Helen Waddell's 1936 *The Desert Fathers* (Constable).

There are a number of biographies of Greta Garbo, perhaps the most famous 'loner' in modern history. The most recent is by David Bret – *Greta Garbo: Divine Star* (Robson Press, 2012).

2. How We Got Here

For the detailed history of the later period of Rome there is the famous (and enormous) *The History of the Decline and Fall of the Roman Empire* by Edward Gibbon (published in six volumes between 1776 and 1781). He was perhaps the first serious historian to blame the fall of Rome on Christianity, which he thought made Romans 'effeminate'.

A more contemporary approach to the specific issues I have been looking at can be found in the works of Professor Peter Brown (of Princeton), who has specialized in the religious culture of the later Roman Empire and early mediaeval Europe. He writes in a way that is wonderfully accessible as well as scholarly. Among his relevant books are: *Augustine of Hippo: A Biography* (University of California Press, 1967); *The Body and Society: Men, Women, and Sexual Renunciation in Early Christianity* (Columbia University Press, 1988) and most recently *Through the Eye of a Needle: Wealth, the Fall of Rome, and the Making of Christianity in the West, 350–550 AD* (Princeton University Press, 2012).

The Eagle of the Ninth Chronicles (OUP, 2010) is a trilogy of children's novels by Rosemary Sutcliff, set in Roman Britain. The third of the series – *The Lantern Bearers* – is an extremely moving account of the resistance to the Saxon invaders after Rome pulled the legions out of Britain to defend the imperial city itself. It addresses the conflict of values and the sense of devastation and cultural unhinging – on all sides – as the Empire declined and broke up.

In Britain at least thirty-six of our present towns and cities, including London, have Roman foundations. Visits to the Roman Baths in Bath (hence the city's name) and the Amphitheatre in Chester both offer a powerful impression of the high value of public and civic life even at the furthest ends of the Empire. A trip that takes in both Hadrian's Wall (and its associated artefacts) and Lindisfarne (the Holy Island) or the Farne Isles, where St Cuthbert (c. 634–687) had his hermitage, shows the contrast between the two ideals very sharply (while also providing some beautiful empty terrain for solitary walking).

The Romantic movement in Britain is best known through its poets: William Wordsworth, Samuel Taylor Coleridge, Lord Byron, Percy Bysshe Shelley and John Keats are perhaps the key names. Wordsworth was the most articulate about the value of solitude and its crucial importance to artists. It is a central and continuing theme of his work. For him solitude in nature was essential to creative inspiration. He has had immeasurable influence on the poetic ideal ever since. His poetry is still widely read and accessible. He is especially associated with the Lake District (Cumbria).

III. Rebalancing Attitudes to Solitude

Professor Robin Dunbar has written about his discoveries in numerous academic papers. But he has also written a general readers' book called *How Many Friends Does One Person Need?: Dunbar's Number and Other Evolutionary Quirks* (Faber & Faber, 2010). Although his work is really about human sociability rather than being alone, it is illuminating and thought-provoking about contemporary social culture. It is fun to read too, as he has a humorous and lively style.

Anne Wareham is a garden writer, and the author of *The Bad Tempered Gardener* (Francis Lincoln, 2011). Her garden at Veddw House in Monmouthshire (www.veddw.com) is one of my favourite in the country – beautiful, original and provocative. It is open to the public.

Catherine of Siena (1347–1380) was a rather extraordinary woman; despite a humble background she became a spiritual mentor to the then Pope and an influential figure in the complicated church politics of her time. She also had intense mystical experiences. Although illiterate, she is one of only four women 'Doctors of the Church' – a title conveyed on saints who have had a profound influence on theology. There are a number of biographies; in the context of understanding her ideas about solitude, *Catherine of Siena* by the Nobel Prize-winning novelist Sigrid Undset (Ignatius Press, 2009 – new edition) is excellent.

1.*Face the Fear*

Mind, the mental-health charity, has a good, practical down-to-earth pamphlet on phobias. If you do find being alone particularly disturbing or anxiety-provoking, or find other people's enjoyment of being alone distasteful or repellent, it is worth reading this and exploring for yourself if your fears are actually a little pathological (www.mind.org.uk/mental_health_a-z/8005_phobias).

To be honest, I personally do not enjoy floatation tanks very much (mainly because I seem to roll over and get a mouthful of vile sali-nated water; but also because I best like my solitude in my house or outside in nature). But I know lots of people who love them. They are available at many beauty and health spas and are a good way of experimenting with being alone in a protected environment.

St Anthony the Great (251–356) is generally regarded as the founder of the Christian hermit tradition. He was an Egyptian Christian who went out to live in the desert. He attracted many followers. Athanasius (296–373), the Bishop of Alexandria, knew him personally and wrote his biography, *The Life of St Anthony*, which describes the early adventures in desert solitude with sympathy and admiration. It is still in print in numerous translations and editions.

Vicki Mackenzie has written a biography of Tenzin Palmo, paying special attention to her long periods of solitude – *Cave in the Snow* (Bloomsbury, 1999). In it she discusses the value and meaning of solitude in a Buddhist context. Palmo herself has commented that she does not know how Mackenzie managed to make a page-turner out of years of sitting in a small cave alone.

2. Do Something Enjoyable Alone

In addition to looking at how you spend your leisure time, it is also interesting to look at your own 'maintenance' time. This is partly because household maintenance is something that not only can be, but often is, done alone. If you are trying to find time for solitude you may already have it if you stop seeing vacuuming as a disagreeable task and see it instead as a period of peaceful solitude; since it has a clear purpose and a definite point of completion, it may even turn out to be a very easy and unscary way of being alone.

3. Explore Reverie

Carl Jung's own book *The Undiscovered Self*, which he wrote to try and explain his ideas to a non-specialist readership, puts my very inadequate description of his notion of 'the active imagination' into a wider theoretical context. Routledge published a new edition in 2002. Anthony Stevens's *Jung: a very short introduction* (Oxford University Press, 2001) is also helpful.

Many people find 'free writing' is a helpful way of accessing this sort of material. Free writing is a technique originally developed to help with 'writer's block' and is advocated by many creative writing guides like Julia Cameron's *The Artist's Way* (Pan, 1992) and Natalie Goldberg's *Writing Down the Bones* (Shambhala Publications, 1986). The basic idea is that you set yourself a time limit (say fifteen minutes or half an hour) and you write, without stopping, whatever comes into your mind. You do not read it until afterwards and you do not correct it. For people who find more traditional reverie difficult or 'pointless', the act of writing seems to provide a focus.

4. Look at Nature

There are so many books about nature – and about specific species – that it is hard to make recommendations. When I really need to remind myself that there is no limit to the bizarre activities that are 'natural', I refer to *The Encyclopedia of Land Invertebrate Behaviour* by Rod and Ken Preston-Mafham (Blandford, 1993), which has beautiful photographs and describes an infinite variety of 'natural' adaptations which allow me to stop worrying about the odd social actions of my acquaintances.

More seriously, Annie Dillard's beautiful book *Pilgrim at Tinker Creek* (Canterbury Press, 2011 – new edition), which won a Pulitzer prize in 1975, addresses these issues and at the same time describes a solitary sojourn in a valley in Virginia, USA.

5. *Learn Something by Heart*

If you haven't learned anything by heart since you left primary school, here are a few easy 'starters': your favourite poem (this is easiest if it rhymes, or at least has a strong regular rhythm); one of Shakespeare's soliloquies; the 7 times-table; the tube stations on the Circle Line; your regular telephone numbers in the order of most frequent use; (part of) Martin Luther King's 1963 'I have a dream' speech.

6. *Going Solo*

If you do not know anyone you can ask directly about solo adventures, there is a wonderful range of books. Here are my top ten (although I have left out some favourites because I have already described them elsewhere in this book). Some are novels.

The Long Way by Bernard Moitessier (Doubleday, 1971). Moitessier was in many ways a natural 'loner', without any pejorative connotations. He was a French single-handed yachtsman and this book is an account of his non-stop solo circumnavigation. When he set out, it was as part of the first Golden Globe Race (which Robin Knox-Johnston won), at which point such a journey had never been accomplished, or even attempted. However, after about two-thirds of the journey, Moitessier decided that he did not want to win the race or even go back to Europe at all, so instead he just sailed on, completing another half-circuit until he reached Tahiti. The book is a lyrical, even mystical, account of the journey and the joys of solitude. It is worth noting that Moitessier was a very experienced and highly skilled sailor, and also a professional writer.

Robinson Crusoe by Daniel Defoe, 1719. This is fiction. It is also one of the great adventure stories of English literature, and is a profound meditation on solitude and both its positive and negative aspects. Of course, in the end Man Friday turns up and Crusoe is no longer alone. If you have only read one of the versions created for children you will be surprised.

Walden; or, Life in the Woods by Henry Thoreau, 1854. Henry Thoreau was an American radical thinker – with some fairly eccentric views on a number of subjects. He went to live alone in a tiny hut in a wood not far from Concord for two years, and wrote this major US classic about it. It is a joyful, rambling book, full of rich description, odd thoughts about life, a philosophy of freedom and a wonderful sardonic commentary on his contemporaries. It may well have inspired the whole movement towards confessional autobiography, and was also a forerunner of the ecology movement. If it does not lead you at the very least to be tempted to try a small taste of solitude, I can only feel sorry for you.

Sea Room by Adam Nicolson (Harper Collins, 2002). Nicolson's father gave him three tiny islands off the west coast of Scotland called the Shiants. Here Nicolson traces their history and their ecology and the patterns of extraordinary and lonely lives lived on them. Although no one is actually 'alone' for very long, the islands themselves are so isolated and far away – not just in space but in atmosphere – that their very existence is somehow an adventure into solitude. Nicolson is a loving biographer and historian, and himself a visitor. Lovely and encouraging and hopeful.

Walking Home by Simon Armitage (Faber & Faber, 2012). The poet Simon Armitage walked the Pennine Way alone in 2010, and this is the account of his journey. It is not an 'adventure' in the sense that some of the other books are – although he made it more challenging by travelling as a troubadour, singing for his supper in pubs and other places en route. But it is a glorious, thoughtful, touching book about some of the pleasures of solitude and the beauties of hill walking.

A Woman in the Polar Night by Christiane Ritter (trans. Jane Degras) (Allen & Unwin, 1954). It probably is not very useful to include this book, because it is very hard to get hold of – but there are so few adventure stories by women, and she writes so extraordinarily well about polar solitude, that I am including it anyway.

Rogue Male by Geoffrey Household (1939, new edition, Orion, 2013). This classic thriller takes solitude to a new level. It is a great adventure story and an extraordinary meditation on solitude, freedom and survival. It is very exciting.

The High Lonesome: Epic Solo Climbing Stories, ed. John Long (Falcon Press, 1999). I don't get it myself, not really; solo rock climbing and mountaineering scare rather than excite me. I first read this to try and understand. Nonetheless Long has collected some thrilling and thoughtful accounts from a range of individuals who do enjoy this high and giddy solitude and are reflective enough to try and explain why.

The Places in Between by Rory Stewart (Picador, 2004). Stewart walked across Afghanistan, alone, just after the Taliban had fallen.

His book is an extraordinary mixture of politics, exploration, travel description and human endurance. It has an odd, rather endearing nineteenth-century feel about it – minimizing discomfort and danger, slightly self-mocking – and introduces a faithful hound. But he writes beautifully about places most of us will never go to. A real adventure.

A Voyage for Madmen by Peter Nichols (Profile, 2001). Nichols's book gives a full account of all nine entrants to the 1968–69 *Sunday Times* Golden Globe Race. There were nine entrants, and only one finished. It provides a genuinely thrilling study of a range of different responses to extreme solitude. Sadly there were no women entrants.

There are of course many other stories of lone rangers – by air and sea, in exotic places and nearer home. After you have read some you should be at least be willing to imagine a small adventure into solitude yourself.

7. Train the Children

I have already discussed Anthony Storr's book *Solitude*. I particularly like the way he sees children as tough, as natural survivors, capable of turning even quite dark experiences into creative and nourishing channels. Richard Louv's book *Last Child in the Woods* (Atlantic, 2009) is an impassioned plea for children to be allowed more experience of solitude, particularly outside in wilder places. The book is annoyingly American in some ways (there is rather a lot of pop-psychology), but his evidence is thoroughly marshalled and the 'child' he describes seems to be much more realistic and attractive than the hyper-delicate, endangered, brittle child of too many child experts' fantasies. Like me, he sees many of the problems that children are currently suffering as related to their lack of solitude – and he uses sociological and psychological research to prove the case; he is particularly persuasive on ADD (attention deficit disorder). Tim Gill, in *No Fear* (Calouste Gulbenkian Foundation, 2007), takes a similar line in a more European context. It is on these books and others that I base my opinion that a lack of solitude – and especially solitude out of doors – is one cause of our children's problems.

Both Philip Pullman and Jack Zipes have published modern translations of the Grimm Brothers' collected fairy stories. I find these better for children than modern retellings, where too often the fear of being alone (along with any parental shortcomings) is written out to 'protect' the child.

Where the Wild Things Are by Maurice Sendak, a picture book for very young children, is one of the best starting places for this sort of literature. It manages to be both funny and serious, the pictures are fabulous and the 'hero' victorious through his own courage.

8. Respect Difference

Recently there have been a number of books addressing this question of why extroversion seems to be valued so much more highly than introversion. Susan Cain's *Quiet: The power of introverts in a world that can't stop talking* (Penguin, 2012) is a popular example and there are many others. My difficulty with most of these books is that they completely accept the totalizing binary division, but simply favour the opposite side: 'it is entirely wonderful to be an introvert and you are somehow superior to the extroverts'. The Myers–Briggs

Personality tests, which make introversion and extroversion a key division, and social dependence on them, has reinforced this oppositional approach. Nonetheless there are interesting differences and they are worth knowing more about.

IV. The Joys of Solitude

1. Consciousness of the Self

Although 'take a yoga class' does not, at first sight, look like homework for solitude, learning the techniques of stillness and awareness really does help to make solitude more comfortable and easier. Yoga is the most accessible of these techniques and can, more than many other religious approaches to meditation, like those of Christianity and Sufism, be separated from its undergirding spiritual theory.

3. Relationship with the Transcendent

There are a vast number of books and films, both serious anthropological studies and sensationalist reportage, about rites of passage. *Anthropology: A Beginner's Guide* by Joy Hendry and Simon Underdown (Oneworld, 2012) seems to me a good introduction; it discusses other forms of solitude and their meanings, and places these ritual practices into a wider social context. It is well-referenced if you want to follow anything up.

4. Creativity

Virginia Woolf's essay 'A Room of One's Own' (1929, new edition: Penguin, 2002) is a famous feminist text. It is also a flamboyant, funny and clever polemic, which is well worth reading if you want to think about creativity, especially in the arts.

For people with no maths (like me) who would like to understand more about the explosive creative period in the 1920s when quantum mechanics was 'discovered', including Heisenberg's contribution, I have written a story called 'On Sneezing an Uncertain Sneeze' in a collection entitled *Moss Witch and Other Stories* (Comma, 2013). All the fictional stories in the book are about science and are accompanied by mini-essays by eminent scientists. Jim Al-Khalili has written 'Three Years That Changed Physics Forever' to go with my story, explaining what Heisenberg and his colleagues were up to and why it mattered so much.

5. Freedom

The Stations of Solitude (Bantam, 1991) by Alice Koller is a book about self-discovery through solitude.

Picture Acknowledgements

The author and publisher would like to thank the following for permission to reproduce the images used in this book:

Page 8 Sara's cottage © Adam Lee Photography

Page 17 *Woman Spinning Thread*, from *Forty-Three Drawings of Neapolitan Costumes*, by Costanzo Castelli, 1786 © Newberry Library / SuperStock

Page 24 Ellen MacArthur Solo World Record Attempt © Liot Vapillion / DPPI via Getty Images

Page 33 Greta Garbo in *Queen Christina*, 1933 © MGM / THE KOBAL COLLECTION

Pages 42–3 Edinburgh New Town © David Robertson / Retna

Page 59 Girl looking through train window © Jekaterina Nikitina / Getty Images

Page 67 Jetsunma Tenzin Palmo © Dongyu Gatsal Ling Nunnery

Pages 72–3 *The Wedding Dance*, c.1566 (oil on panel), by Bruegel, Pieter the Elder (c.1525–69) © Detroit Institute of Arts, USA / City of Detroit Purchase / The Bridgeman Art Library

Page 75 *Shearing the Rams*, 1890 (oil on canvas), by Thomas William Roberts (1856–1931) © National Gallery of Victoria, Melbourne, Australia / The Bridgeman Art Library

Page 77 Sara, coming home © Adam Lee Photography

Page 87 Mountain Gorilla © Konrad Wothe / Getty Images

Page 93 Nine Muses © Hulton Archive / Getty Images

Page 102–3 Beach, near Durness, Scotland © David Henderson / Getty Images

Page 109 Young boy climbing a tree in the woods © Cavan Images / Getty Images

Page 131–2 *The Vigil* (colour litho), by John Pettie (1839–93) (after) © Private Collection / The Stapleton Collection / The Bridgeman Art Library

Page 135 Emily Dickinson © Three Lions / Stringer / Getty Images

Notes

Notes

Notes

TOOLS FOR THINKING

··

A NEW RANGE OF NOTEBOOKS, PENCILS, CARDS
& GIFTS FROM THE SCHOOL OF LIFE

Good thinking requires good tools. To complement our classes, books and therapies, THE SCHOOL OF LIFE now offers a range of stationery products and gifts that are both highly useful and stimulating for the eye and mind.

THESCHOOLOFLIFE.COM
TWITTER.COM/THESCHOOLOFLIFE

If you enjoyed this book, we'd encourage you to check out other titles in the series:

If you'd like to explore more good ideas for everyday life, The School of Life runs a regular programme of classes, weekends, secular sermons and events in London and other cities around the world.

Browse our shop and visit: